SEW CUTE TO CUDDLE

SEW CUTE TO CUDDLE

12 easy soft toy and stuffed animal sewing patterns

MARISKA VOS-BOLMAN

D&C

David and Charles

www.sewandso.co.uk

CONTENTS

INTRODUCTION

Seven years ago I bought a sewing machine and my first creation was a little star-shaped pillow with big eyes. This was the first of many soft toys that I have made since then. After a few years of creating soft toys for family and friends, I decided to share my passion for designing character toys. I started to make sewing patterns and kits, and I named my pattern collections DIY Fluffies. My toys sold very successfully and after so much great feedback, I decided to change my profession from 3D computer modeller to full-time soft-toy creator. So soft-toy making has really changed my life.

When writing this, my first book of soft-toy patterns, I wanted to keep true to those qualities that have made my patterns so successful, in particular the step-by-step tutorials that are generously illustrated each step of the way, making the creation of my soft toys so easy to understand and therefore so enjoyable to make. I have known many beginner sewers make even my most advanced patterns because my tutorials are so detailed, and their results always look great! Also, the actual size patterns I provide mean you can trace them straight off the page and start sewing immediately.

I am often asked what inspires me and the answer is Japanese toys and my two young sons. My approach to my pattern instructions is based on the fantastic detail of Japanese pattern books, where each step is broken down in amazing detail. And, as for the toys themselves, my boys always have great ideas for mummy to make (my oldest son loves Daron the dragon, while my youngest son likes them all!).

So now it is time for a book filled with nothing but DIY Fluffies patterns, and I am very grateful to the team at F+W Media for giving me this opportunity. It is a dream come true. The toys featured in this book have been my secret projects for over a year and I'm very excited that I can finally share them with you. The toy chapters are ordered according to level of difficulty, starting with Joey the bear, a great project for beginners, and ending with Daron the dragon, a more challenging project for more advanced sewers. At the back of the book you'll find the full-size toy patterns as well as information about tools and fabrics, stitching and stuffing techniques, and there are super-helpful tips all along the way. I hope you have as much fun creating these adorable toys as I did designing them.

Emma

Kitty

Mary

Brody

Missy

Joey

Daron

MEET THE GANG

Gronk

Emilio

Wooksy

Patrick

Tyler

JOEY THE BEAR

Joey may be small but make no mistake — he is one brave little bear. Dragons and dinosaurs are his favourite toys and he can growl like a full-grown T-Rex, so prepare to be scared. But who will growl loudest — Joey or his owner? Make one for your little one and find out. This is a very easy sewing project, so it makes the perfect starting point if you are a beginner to soft-toy making.

You will need

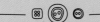

Light brown cotton fabric for the head, legs and arms: 45 x 30cm (18 x 12in)

Blue cotton fabric for the body: 25 x 15cm (10 x 6in)

Black felt for the eyes and nose: 5 x 5cm (2 x 2in)

Small piece white felt for the eye centres

Sewing thread

Toy filling

Basic tool kit (see Tools & Techniques)

1 Make a copy of all the pattern pieces for Joey the bear (see Patterns), remembering to transfer all the pattern markings too; cut out your pattern pieces. Note that the pattern pieces are without seam allowance, so you will need to add a 1cm (⅜in) seam allowance after you draw the pattern on the fabric as required.

2 Working on the wrong side of your fabric, using your pattern pieces and allowing for a 1cm (⅜in) seam allowance, draw and cut out: from the light brown cotton fabric (A), two heads (one reversed), four arms (two reversed), one tail and four legs (two reversed); and from the blue cotton fabric (B), two bodies (one reversed). Draw and cut out the following from the pieces of felt without seam allowance: from the white felt (C), two eye centres; and from black felt (D), two eyes (one reversed) and one nose.

Cutting plan

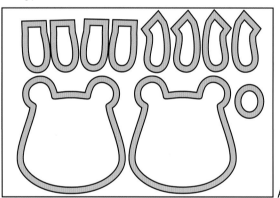

A

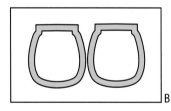

B

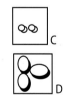

C

D

3 Referring to the markings on the pattern piece, pin and sew the nose and the eyes onto the front of the face. Sew the eye centres onto the eyes. Place the two head pieces together with right sides facing and pin. Sew all the way around the head leaving an opening for the neck. Trim the seam allowance; turn right side out and stuff with toy filling.

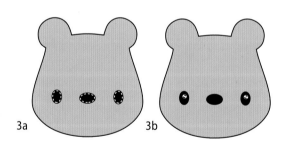

3a   3b

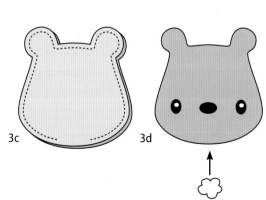

3c   3d

4 Pair up the leg pieces (4a) and the arm pieces (4b) with right sides facing; pin, then sew together leaving the straight edge unstitched. Trim the seam allowances; turn the legs and arms right side out and stuff with toy filling.

6 Take the completed body and push it into the neck opening of the head. Hand sew the front of the body to the front of the face before adding a little more toy filling to the head from the back of the neck, then hand sew the back of the body to the back of the head using ladder stitch (see Stitching Techniques).

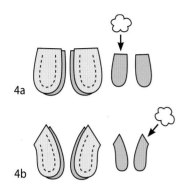

4a

4b

6

5 Place the front and back body pieces together with right sides facing; pin, then sew together leaving openings for the neck, arms and legs as marked on the pattern (5a). Push the arms into the arm holes and sew in place, then push the legs into the leg holes and sew in place (5b). Turn the body right side out and stuff it with toy filling.

TIP: Sewing the front of the body in place first means you can continue to stuff the head with toy filling without the neck bending.

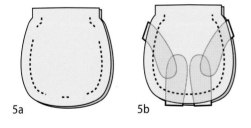

5a

5b

TIP: If you find it hard to sew in the legs as shown in the diagram above, turn the body right side out first, push the legs into the leg holes and hand sew in place with ladder stitch (see Stitching Techniques).

7 Take the tail piece and hand sew a line of large running (gathering) stitches around the edge. Put a little bit of toy filling in the middle and pull up the thread to create the tail, securing the thread with a knot. Ladder stitch the tail onto the back of the body, so that it is centred above Joey's legs (see Stitching Techniques).

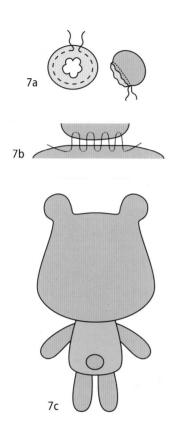

7a

7b

7c

Your bear is made!

TIP: If you want to make Joey a girlfriend, make her up in the same way but use the body of Missy the Koala when cutting out the pattern pieces and make a bow for her hair.

WOOKSY THE OWL

This little sleepy-eyed owl makes the perfect bedtime companion.
He loves to sleep and will only wake up when he is very hungry.
Wooksy is an ideal starter project for those just beginning to sew — he
is easy, fun and fast to make. You'll need some bright-coloured cotton
fabric and felt in several different colours to make this funky bird,
but watch out — once you have made one, you'll want to make more.

You will need

Red cotton fabric for the body and
wings: 45 x 35cm (18 x 14in)

Yellow cotton fabric for the
belly: 10 x 15cm (4 x 6in)

Brown cotton fabric for the
feet: 15 x 20cm (6 x 8in)

White felt for the eyes: 15 x 10cm (6 x 4in)

Black felt for the eye centres: 5 x 10cm (2 x 4in)

Yellow felt for the eyelids: 10 x 10cm (4 x 4in)

Orange felt for the feathers: 10 x 10cm (4 x 4in)

Brown felt for the beak: 5 x 5cm (2 x 2in)

Fusible webbing: 10 x 15cm (4 x 6in)

Sewing thread

Toy filling

Basic tool kit (see Tools & Techniques)

1 Make a copy of all the pattern pieces for Wooksy the owl (see Patterns), remembering to transfer all the pattern markings too; cut out your pattern pieces. Note that the pattern pieces are without seam allowance, so you will need to add the seam allowance after you draw the pattern on the fabric as required.

2 Working on the wrong side of your fabric, using your pattern pieces and allowing for a 1cm (⅜in) seam allowance, draw and cut out: from the red cotton fabric (A), two bodies (one reversed) and four wings (two reversed); and from the brown cotton fabric (B), four feet (two reversed). Draw and cut out the following from the pieces of felt without seam allowance: from white felt (C), two eyes (one reversed); from yellow felt (D), two eyelids (one reversed); from orange felt (E), five feathers; from black felt (F), two eye centres; and from brown felt, one beak (G).

Cutting plan

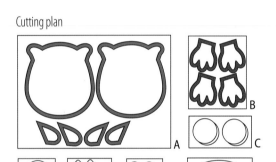

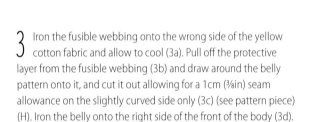

3 Iron the fusible webbing onto the wrong side of the yellow cotton fabric and allow to cool (3a). Pull off the protective layer from the fusible webbing (3b) and draw around the belly pattern onto it, and cut it out allowing for a 1cm (⅜in) seam allowance on the slightly curved side only (3c) (see pattern piece) (H). Iron the belly onto the right side of the front of the body (3d).

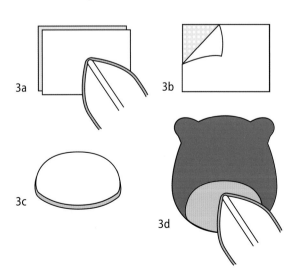

4 Referring to the markings on the pattern piece, pin, then sew the eyes, beak and the feathers onto the front of the body. Sew the eye centres onto the eyes, then place the eyelids on top and sew in place. Secure the belly onto the body using a straight machine stitch or a zigzag stitch; if you use a very narrow zigzag stitch it will give an embroidered effect.

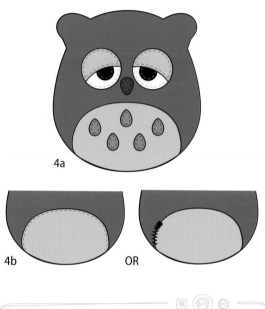

4a

4b   OR

TIP: The pupils are positioned off centre on the eyes to give Wooksy a sleepy-eyed look.

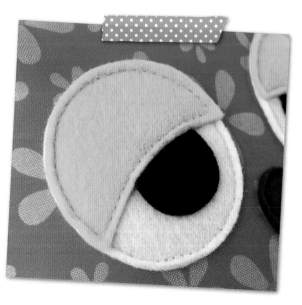

5 Pair up the foot pieces with right sides facing and pin. Sew each pair together leaving the straight edge unstitched. Trim the seam allowances; turn right side out and stuff with toy filling. Make the wings in the same way.

6 Place the two body pieces together with right sides facing. Position the feet and wings in between the body pieces (see pattern for placement) and secure each with a pin or two if necessary. Sew all the way around the body leaving a small opening between the feet. Trim the seam allowance; turn right side out and stuff with toy filling. Hand sew the opening closed with ladder stitch (see Stitching Techniques).

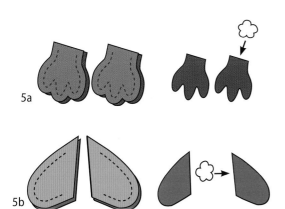

5a

5b

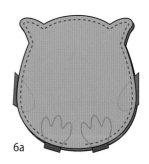

6a

TIP: Clip into the areas between the toes to ensure that Wooksy's feet are nicely shaped when they are turned through.

6b

6c

Your feathered friend
is finished!

MISSY THE KOALA

Missy loves dressing up and there is nothing she likes more than meeting her friends for a tea party. It gives her an excuse to wear her prettiest dress and a bow in her fur. But the party shouldn't last too long because we all know koalas need their beauty sleep! This is a very easy toy to sew and you can make a new friend for your little girl in just a few hours.

You will need

Grey cotton fabric for the head, tail, legs and arms: 35 x 35cm (14 x 14in)

Pink cotton fabric for the body and bow: 25 x 25cm (10 x 10in)

Black felt for the eyes and nose: 10 x 5cm (4 x 2in)

Sewing thread

Toy filling

Basic tool kit (see Tools & Techniques)

Make a copy of all the pattern pieces for Missy the koala (see Patterns), remembering to transfer all the pattern markings too; cut out your pattern pieces. Note that the pattern pieces are without seam allowance, so you will need to add the seam allowance after you draw the pattern on the fabric as required.

2 Working on the wrong side of your fabric, using your pattern pieces and allowing for a 1cm (⅜in) seam allowance, draw and cut out: from the grey cotton fabric (A), two heads (one reversed), four arms (two reversed), one tail and four legs (two reversed); and from the pink cotton fabric (B), two bodies (one reversed), one bow base and one bow centre. Draw and cut out two eyes and one nose from the black felt (C) without seam allowance.

3 Referring to the markings on the pattern piece, pin, then sew the eyes and nose onto the front of the head. Place the two head pieces together with right sides facing and pin. Sew all the way around the head leaving an opening for the neck. Trim the seam allowance; turn the head right side out and stuff with toy filling.

Cutting plan

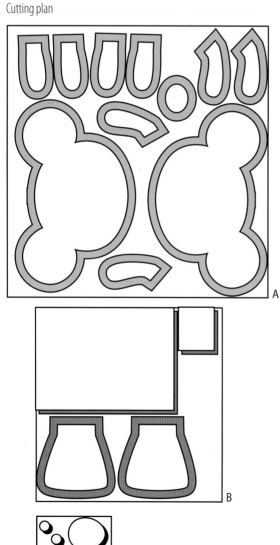

3a

3b

3c

4 Pair up the leg pieces (4a) and the arm pieces (4b) with right sides facing and pin. Sew each pair together leaving the straight edge unstitched. Trim the seam allowances; turn the legs and arms right side out and stuff with toy filling.

6 Turn the body right side out and stuff it with toy filling. Take the completed body and push it into the neck opening of the head. Hand sew the front of the body to the front of the face before adding a little more toy filling to the head from the back of the neck, then sew the back of the body to the back of the head using ladder stitch (see Stitching Techniques).

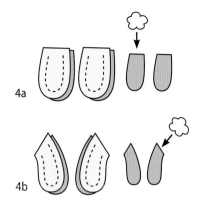

4a

4b

6a

6b

5 Take the front and back body pieces and pin together with right sides facing. Machine stitch together leaving openings for the neck, arms and legs as marked on the pattern. Push the arms into the arm holes and sew in place, then push the legs into the leg holes and sew in place.

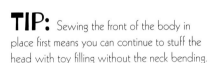

TIP: Sewing the front of the body in place first means you can continue to stuff the head with toy filling without the neck bending.

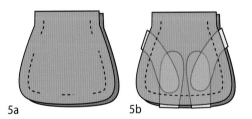

5a

5b

TIP: If you find it hard to sew in the legs as shown in the diagram, turn the body right side out first, push the legs into the leg holes and hand sew in place with ladder stitch (see Stitching Techniques).

7 Take the tail piece and hand sew a line of large running (gathering) stitches around the edge. Put a little bit of toy filling in the middle and pull up the thread to create the tail, securing the thread with a knot. Ladder stitch the tail onto the back of the body, so that it is centred above Missy's legs (see Sewing Techniques).

8 Now make the bow. Take the bow base and fold in half with right sides facing so that the short edges meet and pin in place; sew together with a 1cm (⅜in) seam allowance along the line marked on the bow base pattern (8a). Trim the seam allowance and turn right side out. Position the seam so that it is in the centre at the back (8b), then fold the bow base fabric in half (the seam will be on the outside now). Stitch the short edges with a zigzag stitch (8c); turn right side out and make sure that the zigzagged seam is positioned at centre back (8d).

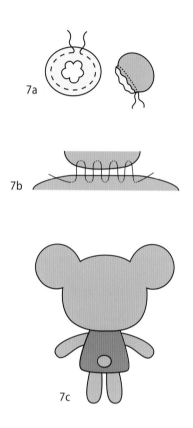

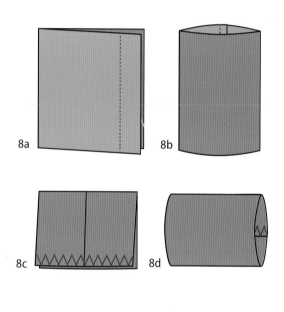

9 The bow centre is made in exactly the same way as the bow base, but it is smaller (see step 8 for more detail).

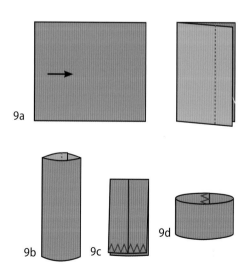

10 To assemble the bow, fold the bow base into three pleats to define its shape. Push the bow centre onto the pleated bow base so that it is positioned in the middle of the bow. Use ladder stitch to attach the bow to Missy's head, angling it across her ear.

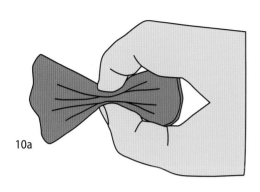

10a

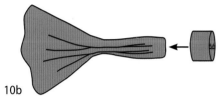

10b

10c

Your koala is complete!

TIP: To make a removable bow, sew the finished bow onto an elastic hairband and slip over Missy's ear — you could make her several different coloured bows.

TIP: If you want to make Missy a boyfriend, make him up in the same way but use the body of Joey the bear when cutting out the pattern pieces and omit the bow!

BRODY THE DOG

Brody is such an adorable pup. His cute face will always cheer you up, and when he is not on your lap enjoying a hug, you'll find him outside chasing butterflies, which is something he just can't resist. Brody is easy to make using a light printed linen for his body and a cute miniature spotty cotton fabric for his ears and patches, but other fabric choices will work well too, for example a fleece or minky fabric will make a very soft dog.

You will need

Light-coloured linen fabric for the body, tail and head: 45 x 45cm (18 x 18in)

Brown cotton fabric for the ears: 20 x 20cm (8 x 8in)

Brown cotton fabric for the patches: 15 x 10cm (6 x 4in)

Black felt for the eyes and nose: 5 x 5cm (2 x 2in)

Fusible webbing: 15 x 10cm (6 x 4in)

Sewing thread

Toy filling

Embroidery thread (floss)

Basic tool kit (see Tools & Techniques)

1 Make a copy of all the pattern pieces for Brody the dog (see Patterns), remembering to transfer all the pattern markings too; cut out your pattern pieces. Note that the pattern pieces are without seam allowance, so you will need to add the seam allowance after you draw the pattern on the fabric as required.

2 Working on the wrong side of your fabric, using your pattern pieces and allowing for a 1cm (⅜in) seam allowance, draw and cut out: from the light-coloured linen fabric (A), two heads (one reversed), two body backs (one reversed), one body belly and one tail; and from the larger piece of brown cotton fabric (B), four ears. Draw and cut out two eyes and one nose from the black felt (C) without seam allowance.

3 Iron the fusible webbing onto the wrong side of the smaller piece of brown cotton fabric and allow to cool (3a). Pull off the protective layer from the fusible webbing (3b) and draw around the three patch pattern pieces onto it (D), and cut them out without seam allowance. Setting aside the two back patches for the time being, iron the face patch onto the head front and machine stitch in place to secure. Sew the felt eyes onto the head front using straight machine stitch.

Cutting plan

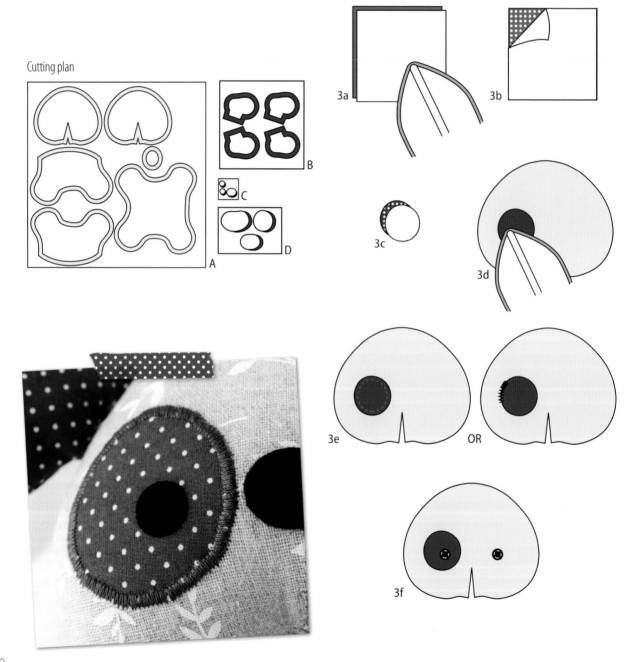

28

4 Pair up the ear pieces with right sides facing and pin. Sew each pair together leaving the straight edge unstitched (4a). Trim the seam allowances; turn right side out and stuff with toy filling (4b).

5 Place the two head pieces together with right sides facing. Position the ears in between the head pieces and pin. Sew all the way around the head but do not sew up the dart. Working on the face side of the head only, sew the dart (see Stitching Techniques). Turn the head right side out through the unstitched dart at the back of the head. Stuff with toy filling and hand sew the dart opening closed with ladder stitch (see Stitching Techniques). Hand sew the nose onto the head with backstitch.

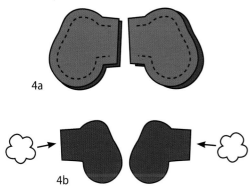

4a

4b

TIP: If you are using very thin fabric, the ears might bend. For a stiffer, stronger ear, add an ear piece cut from fleece (or similar thick fabric) in between the cotton fabric ear pieces.

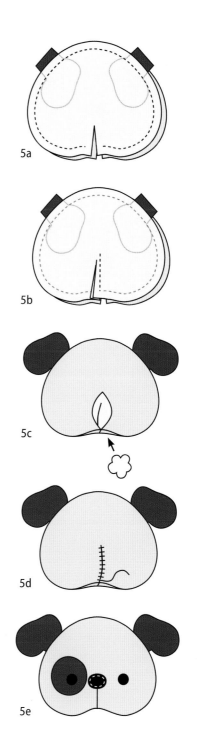

5a

5b

5c

5d

5e

6 Iron back patch 1 onto the right side of the body back (6a) and back patch 2 onto the left side of the body back (6b), and machine stitch in place to secure using straight or zigzag stitch, referring to step 3 for more detail.

7 Place the body back pieces together with right sides facing and pin. Stitch along the top (curved) edge (7a). Open out the joined back piece and place it on top of the body belly with right sides facing. Pin, then sew together leaving an opening at the front for turning (7b). Turn right side out and stuff the body with toy filling (7c). Ladder stitch the turning gap closed (7d).

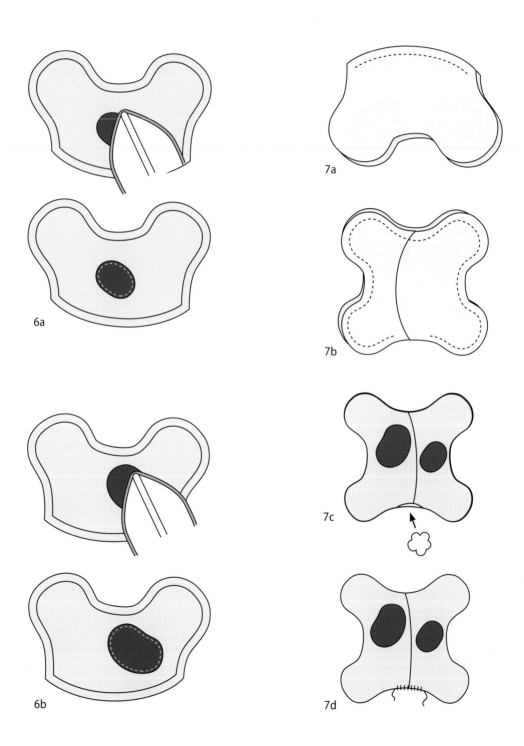

6a

6b

7a

7b

7c

7d

10 To make the claws on Brody's paws, hand sew two long stitches to each using all six strands of embroidery thread. To start, put the needle in at the side of the paw and pull it out at the line that forms the claw, leaving the thread end sticking out; work long straight stitches on top of the paw only. Once complete, trim the thread end.

10

8 Take the tail piece and hand sew a line of large running (gathering) stitches around the edge. Put a little bit of toy filling in the middle and pull up the thread to create the tail, securing the thread with a knot.

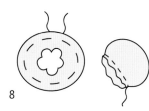

8

9 Ladder stitch the tail and the head onto the body (see Sewing Techniques).

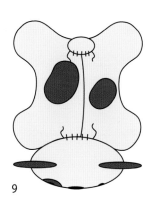

9

Your dog is done!

KITTY THE CAT

Kitty is one of the cuddliest cats you will ever meet. She likes to sleep on a lap all day long and she doesn't mind returning the favour when your little one needs a nap. With her orange print fur and dark orange stripes, she is a marmalade cat, but this soft-toy design is very easy to customize, and she can be made to look like your own cat.

You will need

Orange cotton fabric for the body and the tail: 50 x 60cm (20 x 24in)

Red cotton fabric for the tail: 15 x 15cm (6 x 6in)

Black felt for the eyes and nose: 5 x 10cm (2 x 4in)

Red felt for the stripes: 20 x 25cm (8 x 10in)

Sewing thread

Toy filling

Basic tool kit (see Tools & Techniques)

1 Make a copy of all the pattern pieces for Kitty the cat (see Patterns), remembering to transfer all the pattern markings too; cut out your pattern pieces. Join the pattern pieces for the body. Cut the tail pattern into its component parts remembering to label them tail 1, tail 2, etc and copy all the numbers on the tail pieces as well. Note that the pattern pieces are without seam allowance, so you will need to add the seam allowance after you draw the pattern on the fabric as required.

2 Working on the wrong side of your fabric, using your pattern pieces and allowing for a 1cm (⅜in) seam allowance, draw and cut out: from the orange cotton fabric (A), two bodies (one reversed) and two (one reversed) of tail pieces 1, 3, 5 and 7; and from the red cotton fabric (B), two (one reversed) of tail pieces 2, 4, 6. Use a fabric marker to label the tail pieces (tail 1, tail 1R [reversed], tail 2, tail 2R, etc) as well as the relevant number/letter marking in each corner (1a, 1b, 2a, 2b, etc) as this will help you to join up the tail pieces in step 4. Draw and cut out the following from the pieces of felt without seam allowance: from red felt (C), four of stripe 1 (two reversed) and four of stripe 2 (two reversed); and from black felt (D), two eyes and one nose.

TIP: The cat's tail is pieced from many parts. If you are a beginner sewer, it is easier to make a single colour tail — just cut the tail pattern in one single piece and use to draw out and cut the tail from your chosen fabric. Skip step 4.

3 Referring to the markings on the pattern piece, pin and sew the stripes onto the front and the back of the body pieces, adding the eyes and nose to the front of the body also. Place the stripes so that they align with the raw edges of the body pieces (see diagram).

Cutting plan

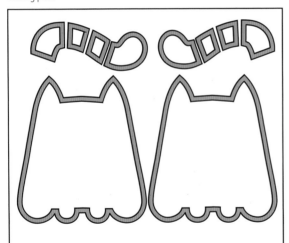

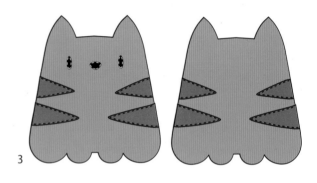

4 Begin to piece the tail. Starting with the piece marked tail 1, place the piece marked tail 2 on top of it with right sides facing, making sure that the number in the corners are the same. Put 2a on 2a, 2b on 2b, etc. Pin together, then sew the line between 2a and 2b (as on diagram 4a). Open out the joined fabric pieces. Do the same for the next piece (tail 3 on tail 2), until you have sewn all the tail pieces together. Repeat to join all the reversed tail pieces in the same way, starting with the piece marked tail 1R and joining it to the piece marked tail 2R.

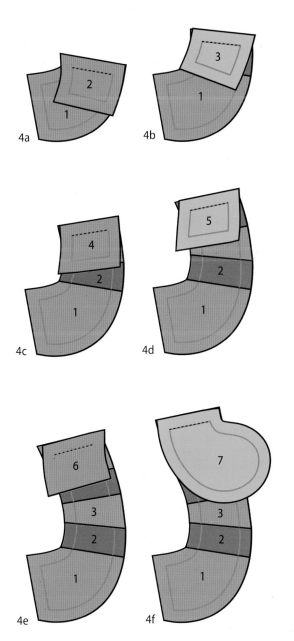

4a

4b

4c

4d

4e

4f

TIP: If you want to create an even more huggable cat, you can use a fur fabric instead of the orange cotton fabric.

5 Take the two pieced tails and place together with right sides facing; pin, then sew together leaving the straight edge open for turning. Trim the seam allowance, turn the tail right side out and stuff it with toy filling. The more toy filling you put into the tail, the more rigid it will be.

TIP: A chopstick is a good tool to help you when stuffing the tail — take small pieces of toy filling and push them into the tail using the chopstick.

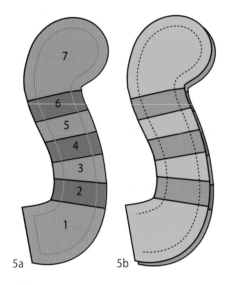

5a   5b

6 Place the back and front body pieces together with right sides facing. Position the tail in between the body pieces (see pattern for placement) and secure with a pin or two if necessary. Sew all the way around the body leaving a small opening between the legs for turning (6a). Trim the seam allowance. Clip into the inner corners of the ears (6b) so that the fabric lies smooth when it is turned.

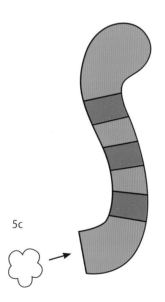

5c

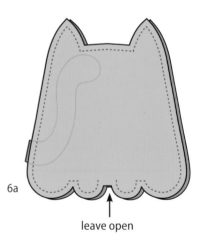

6a

leave open

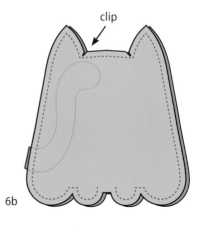

clip

6b

TIP: You can change the colours of your fabrics or add patches to make the toy look like your particular cat. A customized Kitty makes a great gift for cat owners.

7 Turn right side out and stuff the body with toy filling. Hand sew the opening closed with ladder stitch (see Stitching Techniques).

Your cat is created!

7a

7b

EMMA THE GIRL

Lovely Emma likes to play in the garden all day long. She enjoys smelling the flowers, bird watching and playing on her tree swing. Although she is a little bit shy, once you get to know her, there are great adventures to be had together in the garden. Part of the fun of making this doll is picking out the fabrics, from selecting the perfect coloured print for her hair to choosing colourful cottons for her dress and shoes.

You will need

Pink flower-print cotton fabric for the body: 15 x 30cm (6 x 12in)

Cream cotton fabric for the head front and arms: 30 x 30cm (12 x 12in)

Yellow cotton fabric for the head back and bunches: 35 x 30cm (14 x 12in)

Yellow cotton fabric for the fringe (bangs): 25 x 15cm (10 x 6in)

Brown cotton fabric for the legs: 25 x 15cm (10 x 6in)

Red cotton fabric for the feet: 15 x 15cm (6 x 6in)

Black felt for the eyes: 5 x 5cm (2 x 2in)

Red felt for the mouth: 5 x 5cm (2 x 2in)

Fusible webbing: 25 x 15cm (10 x 6in)

Sewing thread

Toy filling

Basic tool kit (see Tools & Techniques)

1 Make a copy of all the pattern pieces for Emma the girl (see Patterns), remembering to transfer all the pattern markings too; cut out your pattern pieces. Note that the pattern pieces are without seam allowance, so you will need to add the seam allowance after you draw the pattern on the fabric as required.

2 Working on the wrong side of your fabric, using your pattern pieces and allowing for a 1cm (⅜in) seam allowance, draw and cut out: from the pink flower-print cotton fabric (A), two bodies (one reversed); from the larger piece of yellow cotton fabric (B), four bunches (two reversed) and one reversed head (head back); from the cream cotton fabric (C), one head (head front) and four arms (two reversed); from the brown cotton fabric (D), four legs (two reversed); and from the red cotton fabric (E), four feet (two reversed). Draw and cut out the following from the pieces of felt without seam allowance: from red felt (F), one mouth; and from black felt (G), two eyes (one reversed).

3 Iron the fusible webbing onto the wrong side of the smaller piece of yellow cotton fabric (H) and allow to cool. Pull off the protective layer from the fusible webbing and draw around the fringe (bangs) pattern onto it, and cut it out allowing for a 1cm (⅜in) seam allowance on one side only (see pattern piece). Iron the fringe (bangs) onto the right side of the face (see Tools & Techniques).

Cutting plan

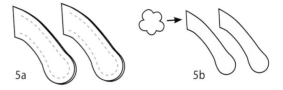

5 Pair up the arm pieces with right sides facing and pin; sew each arm together leaving the straight edge unstitched. Trim the seam allowances; turn the arms right side out and stuff with toy filling.

5a   5b

6 Pair up the hair bunch pieces with right sides facing and pin; sew together leaving the straight edges unstitched. Trim the seam allowances; turn the bunches right side out and stuff with toy filling.

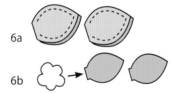

6a

6b

4 Secure the fringe (bangs) onto the head front using a regular straight machine stitch or a zigzag stitch; if you use a very narrow zigzag stitch it will give an embroidered effect. Sew the eyes and mouth in position beneath the fringe (bangs) using straight machine stitch.

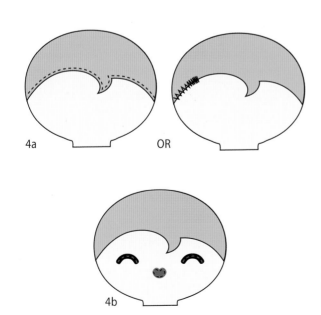

4a   OR

4b

8 Pair up the joined foot/leg pieces with right sides facing and pin; sew together leaving the straight edge unstitched. Trim the seam allowances; turn the legs right side out and stuff with toy filling.

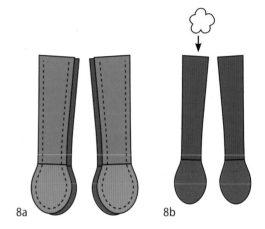

8a

8b

7 Take a foot piece and place it onto the bottom (narrower) end of one of the leg pieces, right sides facing; pin and sew together. Repeat for the remaining foot and leg pieces to give you four joined foot/leg pieces.

9 Place one body piece at the neck of the front of the head with right sides facing; pin, then sew together along the neck (9a). Repeat to stitch the second body piece to the back of the head (9b).

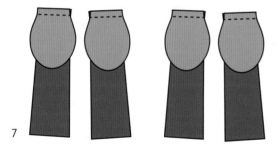

7

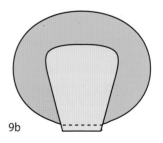

9a

9b

TIP: This doll is very easy to customize. You can replace the bunches with a ponytail, change the shape of the fringe (bangs), alter the size of the mouth, to make many different dolls.

10 Place the two joined head/body pieces together with right sides facing, pin and stitch together, leaving openings for the legs, bunches and arms as marked on the pattern and a small opening at one side of the body for turning (10a). Push the bunches into the openings on the head and sew in place, then push the arms into the arm holes and sew in place, and finally push the legs into the leg holes and sew in place (10b).

11 Trim the seam allowance, turn right side out and stuff the body with toy filling. Hand sew the opening closed with ladder stitch (see Stitching Techniques).

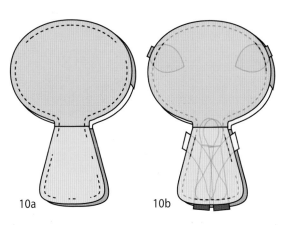

10a   10b

11a   11b

Your doll is done!

TIP: If you find it hard to sew in the legs as shown in the diagram, turn the body right side out first, push the legs into the leg holes and hand sew in place with ladder stitch (see Stitching Techniques).

EMILIO THE BOY

Emilio is an adventurer. Nattily dressed in a colourful T-shirt and summer shorts, he is always ready to scout for animals in the wild. He loves all creatures, except bees that take too much interest in his sweets! This is a great project for the intermediate sewer, and it is so much fun finding small-scale prints for Emilio's outfit and his sweet little sandals.

You will need

Mid brown cotton fabric for the head front, legs and arms: 30 x 45cm (12 x 18in)

Dark brown cotton fabric for the head back and hair tuft: 25 x 25cm (10x 10in)

Dark brown cotton fabric for the fringe (bangs): 25 x 15cm (10 x 6in)

Green patterned cotton fabric for the top: 25 x 10cm (10 x 4in)

Blue patterned cotton fabric for the shorts: 15 x 15cm (6 x 6in)

Dark brown patterned cotton fabric for the feet: 15 x 15cm (6 x 6in)

Black felt for the eyes and mouth: 10 x 5cm (4 x 2in)

Fusible webbing: 25 x 15cm (10 x 6in)

Sewing thread

Toy filling

Basic tool kit (see Tools & Techniques)

1 Make a copy of all the pattern pieces for Emilio the boy (see Patterns), remembering to transfer all the pattern markings too; cut out your pattern pieces. Note that the pattern pieces are without seam allowance, so you will need to add the seam allowance after you draw the pattern on the fabric as required.

2 Working on the wrong side of your fabric, using your pattern pieces and allowing for a 1cm (⅜in) seam allowance, draw and cut out: from mid brown cotton fabric (A), one head (head front), four arms (two reversed) and four legs (two reversed); from the larger piece of dark brown cotton fabric (B), two hair tufts (one reversed) and one reversed head (head back); from the green patterned cotton fabric (C), two tops (one reversed); from the blue patterned cotton fabric (D), two shorts (one reversed); and from the dark brown patterned cotton fabric (E), four feet (two reversed). Draw and cut out two eyes (one reversed) and one mouth from the black felt (F) without seam allowance.

3 Iron the fusible webbing onto the wrong side of the smaller piece of dark brown cotton fabric (G) and allow to cool. Pull off the protective layer from the fusible webbing and draw around the fringe (bangs) pattern onto it, and cut it out allowing for a 1cm (⅜in) seam allowance on one side only (see pattern piece). Iron the fringe (bangs) onto the right side of the face (see Tools & Techniques).

Cutting plan

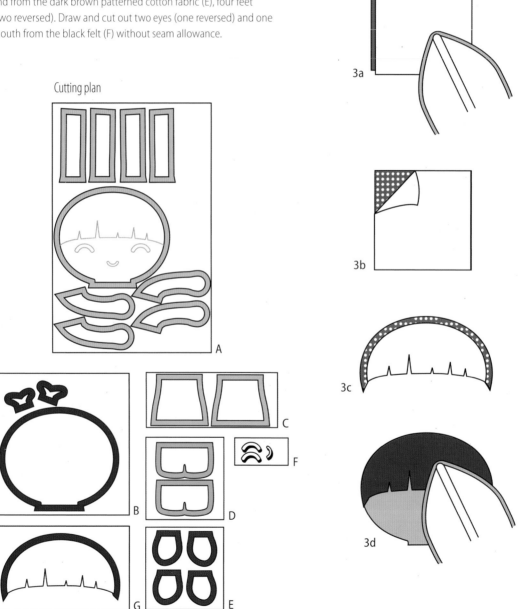

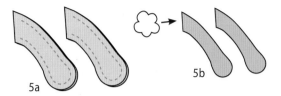

5 Pair up the arm pieces with right sides facing and pin; sew each arm together leaving the straight edge unstitched. Trim the seam allowances; turn the arms right side out and stuff with toy filling.

5a   5b

6 Place the hair tuft pieces together with right sides facing and pin; sew leaving the straight edge unstitched. Trim the seam allowance; turn the hair tuft right side out.

6

4 Secure the fringe (bangs) onto the head front using a regular straight machine stitch or a zigzag stitch; if you use a very narrow zigzag stitch it will give an embroidered effect. Sew the eyes and mouth in position beneath the fringe (bangs) using straight machine stitch.

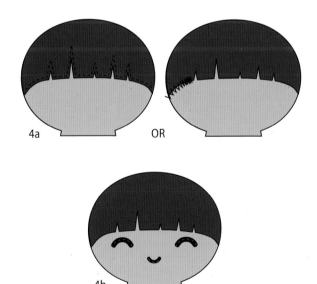

4a   OR

4b

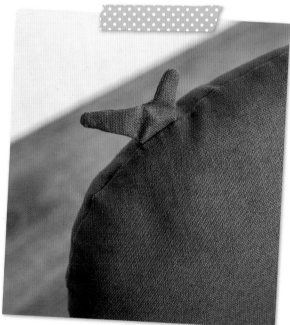

8 Pair up the joined foot/leg pieces with right sides facing and pin; sew together leaving the straight edge unstitched. Trim the seam allowances; turn the legs right side out and stuff with toy filling.

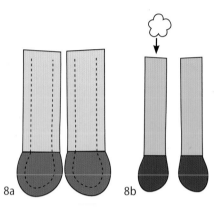

8a   8b

7 Take a foot piece and place it onto the bottom (narrower) end of one of the leg pieces, right sides facing; pin, then sew together. Repeat for the remaining foot and leg pieces to give you four joined foot/leg pieces.

9 The shorts and tops are joined to make the body pieces. Take one shorts piece and place on top of the wider end of a top piece with right sides facing; pin, then stitch together (see diagram). Open out and press seam open. Repeat to make a second body piece.

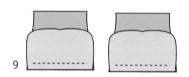

9

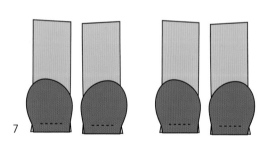

7

TIP: To make a younger brother to look up to Emilio, resize the pattern by 75%. You could also make a friend for him using the girl doll pattern in this book.

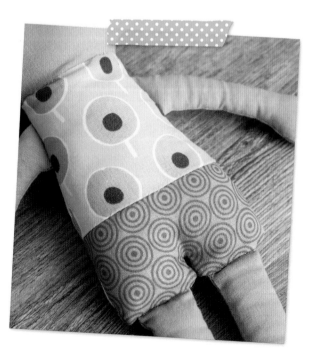

10 Place one joined body piece at the neck of the front of the head with right sides facing and pin; sew together along the neck (10a). Repeat to stitch the second joined body piece to the back of the head (10b).

12 Trim the seam allowance, turn right side out and stuff the body with toy filling. Hand sew the opening closed with ladder stitch (see Stitching Techniques).

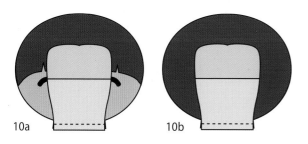

10a 10b

11 Place the two joined head/body pieces together with right sides facing; pin, then stitch together, leaving openings for the legs, hair tuft and arms as marked on the pattern and a small opening at one side of the body for turning (11a). Push the hair tuft into the opening on the head and sew in place, then push the arms into the arm holes and sew in place, and finally push the legs into the leg holes and sew in place (11b).

12a 12b

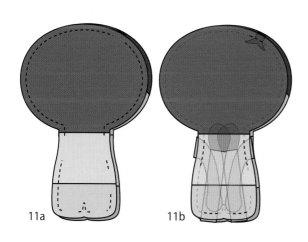

11a 11b

TIP: If you find it hard to sew in the legs as shown in the diagram, turn the body right side out first, push the legs into the leg holes and hand sew in place with ladder stitch (see Stitching Techniques).

Your fabric friend is finished!

GRONK THE MONSTER

Gronk has a dazzling set of white pointed teeth, perfect for polishing off his breakfast, dinner and tea. What a big appetite this furry fellow has — he is hungry all the time and a home-baked blueberry cupcake is his favourite snack. Made from fur fabric, he is extremely huggable. You'll be surprised at just how easy fur fabric is to sew with, but do keep your vacuum cleaner at hand to tidy away the hairiness!

You will need

Purple fur fabric for the body:
50 x 30cm (20 x 12in)

White cotton fabric for the horns and
teeth: 25 x 30cm (10 x 12in)

Green cotton fabric for the arms and
legs: 50 x 40cm (20 x 16in)

Black cotton fabric for the
mouth: 5 x 20cm (2 x 8in)

Black felt for the eyes: 5 x 5cm (2 x 2in)

Sewing thread

Toy filling

Basic tool kit (see Tools & Techniques)

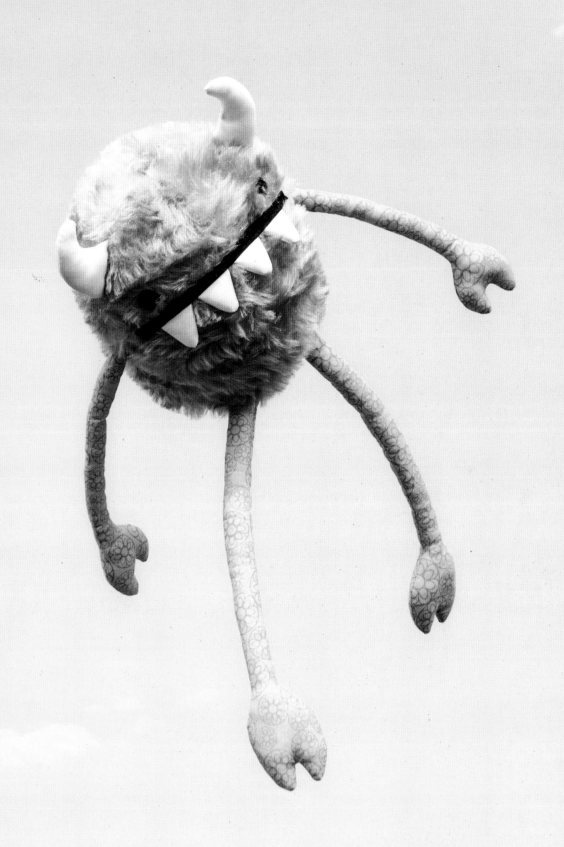

1 Make a copy of all the pattern pieces for Gronk the monster (see Patterns), remembering to transfer all the pattern markings too; cut out your pattern pieces. Note that the pattern pieces are without seam allowance, so you will need to add the seam allowance after you draw the pattern on the fabric as required.

2 Working on the wrong side of your fabric, using your pattern pieces and allowing for a 1cm (⅜in) seam allowance, draw and cut out: from the purple fur fabric (A), two body front pieces (one reversed), two body back pieces (one reversed) and one base; from the green cotton fabric (B), four arms (two reversed) and four legs (two reversed); from the white cotton fabric (C), eight teeth (four reversed) and four horns (two reversed). From the black cotton fabric (D), draw and cut out one mouth without seam allowance. Draw and cut out two eyes from the black felt (E) without seam allowance.

Cutting plan

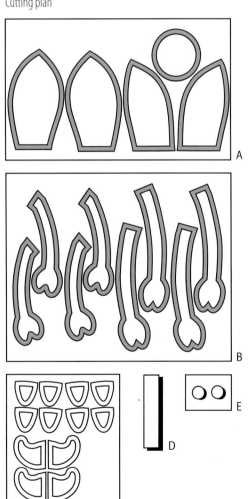

3 Pair up the tooth pieces with right sides facing and pin; sew together leaving the straight edge unstitched. Trim the seam allowances; turn the teeth right side out and stuff with toy filling (3a). Make the horns in the same way (3b).

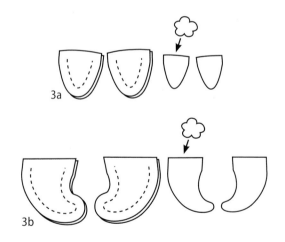

3a

3b

4 Pair up the leg pieces and the arm pieces with right sides
   facing and pin; sew each pair together leaving the straight
edge unstitched. Trim the seam allowances; turn the arms (4a)
and legs (4b) right side out and stuff with toy filling.

TIP: Use a chopstick for turning small parts, such as arms and legs. See Stitching Techniques for detailed instructions.

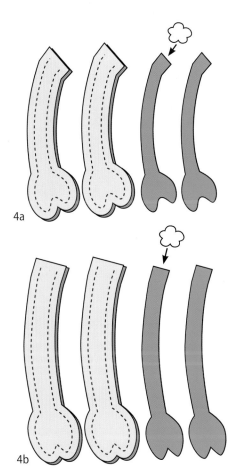

4a

4b

5 Sew the eyes onto the body front pieces (5a). Place the body
   front pieces together with right sides facing and sew along
the front side (see 5b and pattern piece).

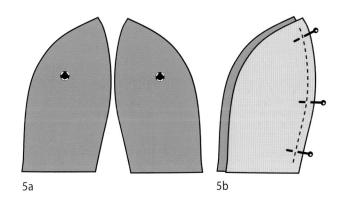

5a   5b

6 Place the body back pieces together with right sides facing
   and sew along the back side (see diagram and pattern piece).

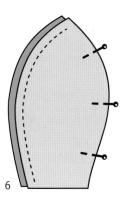

6

7 Open out the body front and the body back. Before placing the body pieces together with right sides facing, make sure that most of the fur has been combed down to lie inside the body. Pin, then stitch the body pieces together, leaving the straight edge unstitched and openings for the arms and horns as marked on the pattern (7a). Push the arms and horns into the appropriate holes, pin, then sew in place (7b).

9 Turn the body right side out and stuff it with toy filling. Hand sew the opening closed with ladder stitch.

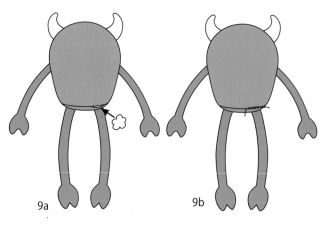

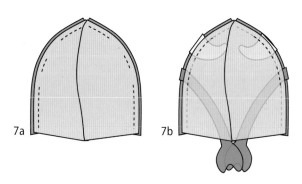

7a   7b

9a   9b

8 Place the base piece at the opening at the bottom of the body and pin in place. Stitch the base to the body, leaving openings for the legs and a larger opening for turning (8a). Push the legs into the leg holes and machine stitch in place (8b).

TIP: If some of the fur is sticking inside the body, you can pull it out gently with a pin or needle.

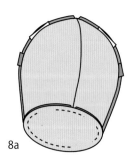
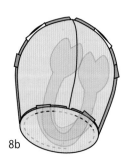

8a   8b

TIP: If you find it hard to sew in the legs as shown in the diagram, turn the body right side out first, push the legs into the leg holes and hand sew in place with ladder stitch (see Stitching Techniques).

11 Sew the finished mouth onto the monster's face by hand using backstitch (see Sewing Techniques).

11

10 Take the mouth piece and, with the wrong side facing you, fold it over at the bottom edge to meet the centre line marked on the pattern; press the fold (10a). Now put the teeth on top of the folded fabric, pin and sew in place (10b). Fold over the top edge of the mouth piece to the centre line and press (10c). Fold in at the sides (10d: see dotted lines on pattern), then fold over the top edge of the fabric to overlay the top (sewn) edge of the teeth and topstitch along the top of the teeth to secure in place (10e).

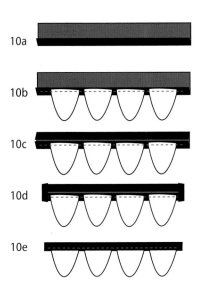

10a

10b

10c

10d

10e

Your monster is made!

PATRICK THE MONKEY

This funny chimp is extremely curious, which often gets him into trouble, but luckily, because of his charming character, Patrick is forgiven very easily. The machine appliqué details for the face, ears and bellybutton are secured with a simple zigzag stitch to give this toy a nice embroidered effect. You could make a whole family of monkeys by just changing the size of the ears a little to make each one different.

You will need

Brown cotton fabric for the legs, arms, body, ears, tail, upper face and head: 55 x 55cm (22 x 22in)

Tan cotton fabric for the ears, middle face and belly: 15 x 15cm (6 x 6in)

Tan cotton fabric for the lower face: 25 x 15cm (10 x 6in)

Black felt for the eyes, nostrils and bellybutton: 5 x 5cm (2 x 2in)

Fusible webbing: 15 x 15cm (6 x 6in)

Sewing thread

Toy filling

Basic tool kit (see Tools & Techniques)

1 Make a copy of all the pattern pieces for Patrick the monkey (see Patterns), remembering to transfer all the pattern markings too; cut out your pattern pieces. Note that the pattern pieces are without seam allowance, so you will need to add the seam allowance after you draw the pattern on the fabric as required.

2 Working on the wrong side of your fabric, using your pattern pieces and allowing for a 1cm (⅜in) seam allowance, draw and cut out: from the brown cotton fabric (A), one upper face, one head, two bodies (one reversed), two tails (one reversed), four ears (two reversed), four legs (two reversed), and four arms (two reversed); and from the larger piece of tan cotton fabric (B), two lower faces (one reversed). Draw and cut out two eyes, two nostrils and one bellybutton from the black felt (C) without seam allowance.

Cutting plan

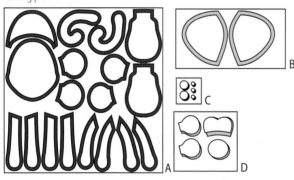

3 Iron the fusible webbing onto the wrong side of the smaller piece of tan cotton fabric (D) and allow to cool. Pull off the protective layer from the fusible webbing and draw out two inner ears (one reversed) and one belly both without seam allowance, and one middle face allowing for a 1cm (⅜in) seam allowance along the lower (slightly curved) edge only (see pattern piece). Cut out the pieces and set aside the belly piece for the time being.

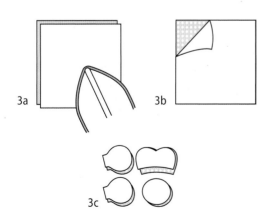

4 To make the front of the ears, iron an inner ear piece onto the right side of an ear piece (4a) and secure in place with a straight machine stitch or a zigzag stitch, using a very narrow zigzag stitch if you want to achieve an embroidered effect (4b). Pair up the ear fronts with the remaining ear pieces with right sides facing and pin; sew the ears together leaving the straight edge unstitched. Trim the seam allowances (4c); turn the ears right side out and stuff with toy filling (4d).

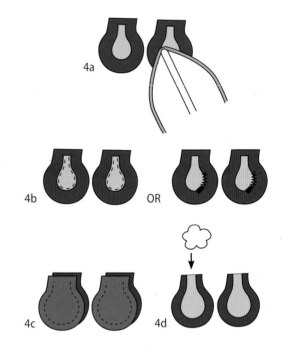

5 Iron the middle face onto the right side of the upper face and machine stitch in place with a straight or zigzag stitch. If you use a very narrow zigzag stitch it will give an embroidered effect. Sew the felt eyes onto the face using straight stitch.

5a

5b   OR

5c

7 Open out the joined face and place the head piece (back of head) on top of it with right sides facing. Position the ears in between the face and head pieces making sure that the front side of the ears are right sides together with the joined face. Pin in place. Sew the head together leaving the neck opening at the base of the head (7a). Turn right side out and stuff the head with lots of toy filling (see Stuffing Techniques).

6 Sew the nostrils onto the lower face pieces (6a). Place the lower face pieces with right sides facing; pin and sew together along the slightly curved edge only (6b). Open out the joined lower face; pin the upper face to the top edge of the lower face with right sides facing and sew together (6c).

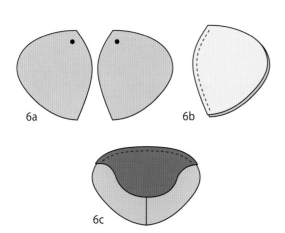

6a   6b

6c

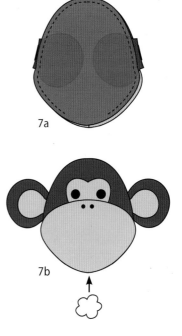

7a

7b

8 Pair up the leg pieces and the arm pieces with right sides
   facing. Pin, then sew together leaving the straight edge
unstitched. Trim the seam allowances; use a chopstick to turn the
legs and arms right side out (see Stitching Techniques) and stuff
with toy filling. Make the tail in the same way and once it has
been stuffed (8f), hand sew the opening closed with ladder stitch.

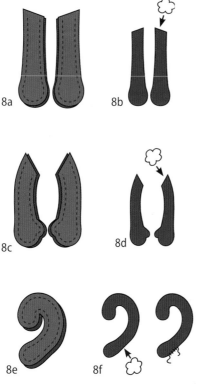

10 Take the front and back body pieces and pin together with
    right sides facing. Machine stitch together leaving openings
for the neck, arms and legs as marked on the pattern. Push the
arms into the arm holes and sew in place, then push the legs into
the leg holes and sew in place. Turn the body right side out and
stuff it with toy filling.

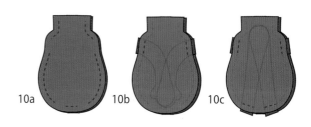

9 Taking the set-aside belly piece, iron it to the right side of one
   of the body pieces. Allow it to cool before securing in place
with a straight machine stitch or a zigzag stitch, using a very
narrow zigzag stitch if you want to achieve an embroidered effect.
Sew the felt bellybutton onto the belly.

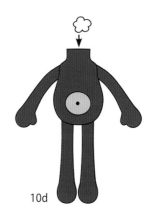

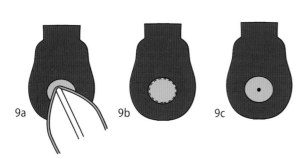

TIP: Make sure that you ladder stitch a large section of the tail onto the body when you are attaching it in place. That way it will be much more secure for swinging from trees or from little one's hands!

12 Take the completed body and push it into the neck opening of the head. Hand sew the front of the body to the front of the face (12a) before adding a little more toy filling to the head from the back of the neck (12b), then sew the back of the body to the back of the head using ladder stitch (12c).

11 Hand sew the tail onto the back of the monkey using ladder stitch (see Stitching Techniques), taking care to make sure that the tail is centred.

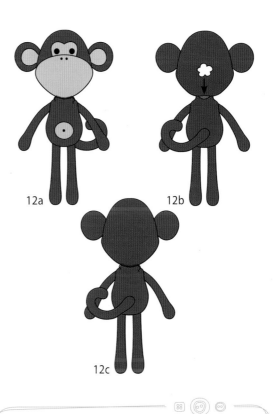

12a   12b

12c

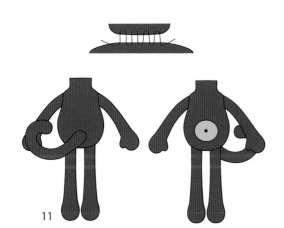

11

TIP: Sewing the front of the body in place first means you can continue to stuff the head with toy filling without the neck bending.

Your monkey is made!

TYLER THE TIGER

Spread-eagled on the floor, Tyler may look like a lazy fellow but put on some funky music and he makes the best dance partner — his fancy moves will surprise you. With his dart-shaped muzzle, pieced tail and many appliqué stripes, Tyler is a little challenging to make, but there are lots of detailed illustrations to guide you, and, while he may take a little more time, he is definitely worth it.

You will need

Orange cotton fabric for the face, head, back, tail, legs and outer ears: 55 x 50cm (22 x 20in)

White cotton fabric for the belly, legs, muzzle and inner ears: 40 x 45cm (16 x 18in)

White cotton fabric for the claws: 15 x 15cm (6 x 6in)

Black cotton fabric for the tail: 10 x 20cm (4 x 8in)

Black felt for stripes, nose and eyes: 30 x 30cm (12 x 12in)

Sewing thread

Toy filling

Embroidery thread

Basic tool kit (see Tools & Techniques)

1 Make a copy of all the pattern pieces for Tyler the tiger (see Patterns), remembering to transfer all the pattern markings too; cut out your pattern pieces. Note that the pattern pieces are without seam allowance, so you will need to add the seam allowance after you draw the pattern on the fabric as required.

2 Working on the wrong side of your fabric, using your pattern pieces and allowing for a 1cm (⅜in) seam allowance, draw and cut out: from the orange cotton fabric (A), two back pieces (one reversed), two ears (one reversed), two side faces (one reversed), one upper face, one lower face, one head, one tail 1 piece, two tail 3 pieces and four legs; from the large piece of white cotton fabric (B), two ears (one reversed), four reversed legs, one belly, one muzzle 1 and one muzzle 2; from the black cotton fabric (C), two tail 2 pieces and one tail 4 piece. Draw and cut out the following from the black felt (D) without seam allowance: two eyes, one nose, eight leg stripe pieces, four stripe 1 pieces (two reversed), two stripe 2 pieces (two reversed), four stripe 3 pieces (two reversed), four stripe 4 pieces (two reversed), four stripe 5 pieces (two reversed) and two stripe 6 pieces (one reversed). (Note: the small piece of white cotton fabric will be used to make the claws in step 7.)

TIP: To make Tyler, there are lots of pieces to cut and sew, and it is a good idea to label them as you cut them out and to keep piles of the same pieces, for example all the leg stripes, together.

3 Referring to the markings on the pattern piece, pin and sew all the black felt pieces onto the relevant orange cotton fabric pieces (side face 3a, head 3b, back 3c and 3d, legs 3e and upper face 3f) and, onto the white cotton fabric, the muzzle 1 (3g), using straight stitch (see Stitching Techniques).

Cutting plan

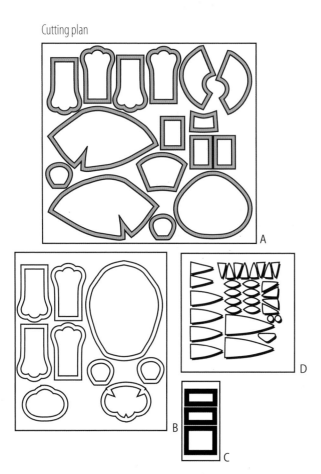

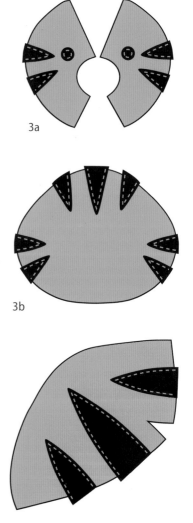

3a

3b

3c

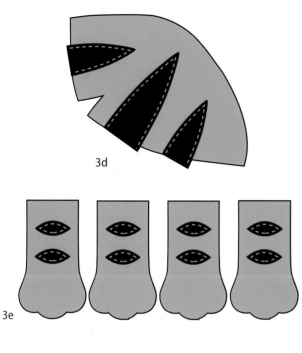

3d

3e

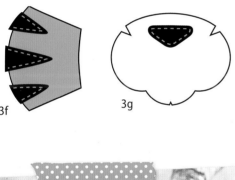

3f

3g

4 Sew the darts on each of the back pieces (see Stitching Techniques).

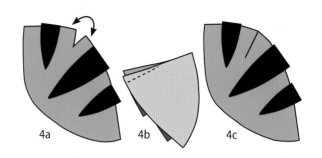

4a 4b 4c

5 Place the orange legs on the back pieces with right sides facing as shown in the diagram; pin, then sew along the straight line of the leg only, to attach each leg to the back pieces.

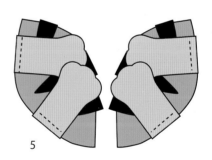

5

6 Place the white legs on the belly piece with right sides facing as shown in the diagram; pin, then sew along the straight line of the leg only to attach each leg to the belly.

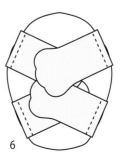

6

7 Now make the claws. Take the small piece of white cotton fabric and cut it in half; pin together with right sides facing. Use the claw pattern piece to draw 12 claws onto the pinned fabric. Sew around the outline of the claws leaving the straight edge unstitched. Cut the claws out close to the stitching line and turn right side out.

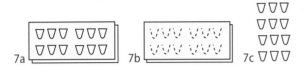

9 Now shape the tail: fold the pieced tail fabric in half with right sides facing and pin; sew from the fold at the tail 4 end rounding the corners of the tail on both sides to create a nice shape, and continuing to sew along the edge to the tail 1 end, leaving this end open for turning (9a). Trim the seam allowance and turn the tail right side out. Put a bit of toy filling in the tail, but not too much or your tail will be very stiff.

8 Now piece the tail. Take tail 1 and position a tail 2 piece on top with right sides facing (8a). Pin and sew together along one side as shown in the diagram. Open out the joined fabric pieces and place a tail 3 piece on top with right sides facing (8b); pin, sew and open out. Continue in the same way, adding the second tail 2 piece (8c), then the second tail 3 piece (8d), and finally the tail 4 piece (8e), remembering to open it out (8f).

TIP: If you want the tiger's tail to be heavy, use a heavy stuffing in the bottom of the tail, such as plastic pellet filling (see Stuffing Techniques).

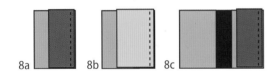

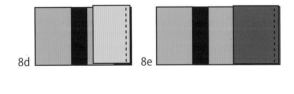

10 Place the back pieces together with right sides facing, sandwiching the tail in between in the position marked on the pattern. Pin, sew along the top edge (see diagram), then open out.

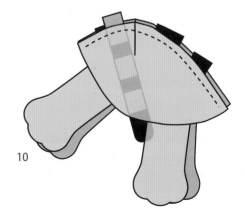

11 Now place the joined back and belly together, with right sides facing and sandwich the claws (with the pointed ends facing inwards) in between the layers at the ends of the legs, pinning everything in place. Sew all the way around the edge leaving a small opening at the neck. Trim the seam allowance; turn right side out and stuff with toy filling, starting with the legs.

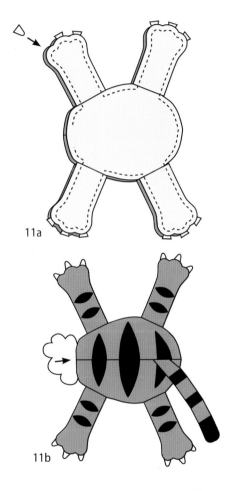

11a

11b

TIP: When stuffing the tiger's body, leave a bit of room where the leg meets the body, so that the legs can still move.

TIP: Generally, I stitch the claw details onto the paws in step 19, but you could do it before stuffing the body if you prefer. Knot the end of the embroidery thread and take the needle through the fabric from the inside, sew the claws, then take the needle and thread back inside the body and sew a few stitches on the seam allowance to make sure it is secured.

12 Now stitch the face together, starting with the orange fabric pieces. Pin and sew the right-hand side face onto the right-hand side of the upper face with right sides facing (12a), then join the left-hand side face onto the left-hand side of the upper face in the same way (12b). Now pin and sew on the lower face to either side at the base of the face (12c and 12d). You now have a tiger's face with a big hole in the middle where the muzzle will go (12e).

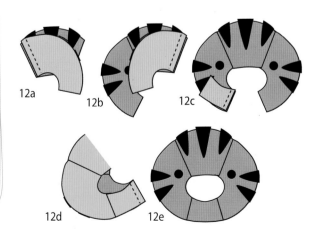

12a

12b

12c

12d

12e

13 To make the muzzle, begin by sewing the darts on muzzle 1 (see Stitching Techniques). Start with the darts at either side of the nose (13b), then stitch the dart at the chin (13c).

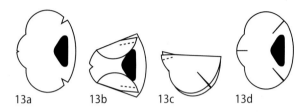

13a   13b   13c   13d

14 Now take muzzle 1 and pin it on top of muzzle 2 with WRONG sides facing; sew all around the edge (14a). Cut a small slit on the back of the muzzle (14b) and put a little toy filling into the chin (leave the slit open). Machine stitch the mouth lines (see pattern and 14c) – if this is proving difficult, you may have put too much stuffing in the chin!

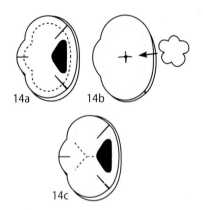

14a   14b

14c

15 Now sew the completed muzzle into the hole in the tiger's face. You might find this easier to do by hand. Pin the muzzle into the hole first before you start sewing. When you have completed the sewing of the muzzle into the tiger's face you can put some more toy filling into the muzzle using a chopstick to ease it carefully through the slit.

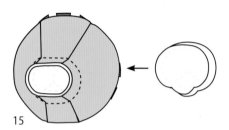

15

16 Pair up the orange (outer) ear pieces with the white (inner) ear pieces with right sides facing. Pin, then sew together leaving the straight edge unstitched. Trim the seam allowances and turn the ears right side out. Fold each ear in half at the bottom edge and sew together by hand.

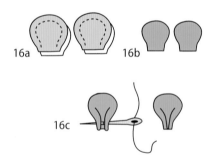

16a   16b

16c

17 Place the tiger's face on top of the head piece with right sides facing; pin, then sew together around the edge, leaving small openings for the ears and a larger opening at the neck for turning. Trim the seam allowance and turn right side out.

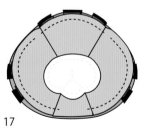

17

18 Push the ears into the ear openings and hand sew the ears in place with ladder stitch (see Stitching Techniques). Fill the head with lots of toy filling, then hand sew the opening closed with ladder stitch.

20 Hand sew the head onto the body using ladder stitch. Try different head placements before you stitch it on to see which you prefer – a straight-on look or a quizzical tilt of the head.

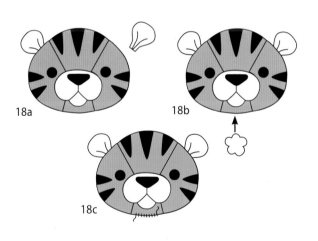

18a 18b 18c

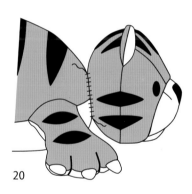

20

19 To define the claws on Tyler's paws, hand sew four long stitches in between using the embroidery thread. Start by putting the embroidery needle in at the side of the feet and pull it out at the line that forms the claws. Leave some thread sticking out of the feet until you have finished the embroidery, then cut it off.

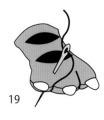

19

Your tiger is complete!

MARY THE HIPPO

Mary is the perfect companion for little artists as she is a very creative hippo. Forget finger-painting — she loves to make beautiful mud paintings with her big feet! To make this crafty creature, you'll need to stock up on the toy filling, as she is very big and round. A pair of glass eyes makes Mary look so cute, but these can be replaced with felt or fleece eyes for babies and very young children.

You will need

Flower-print cotton fabric for the body, head, belly, legs, tail and outer ears: 70 x 65cm (28 x 26in)

Lilac cotton fabric for the inner ears: 20 x 10cm (8 x 4in)

Wadding (batting) for the ears: 20 x 10cm (8 x 4in)

Lilac felt for the nostrils: 10 x 10cm (4 x 4in)

Glass, plastic or felt eyes: 18mm (¾in)

Sewing thread

Toy filling

Basic tool kit (see Tools & Techniques)

1 Make a copy of all the pattern pieces for Mary the hippo (see Patterns), remembering to transfer all the pattern markings too; cut out your pattern pieces. Join the pattern pieces for the body back, body side and head front. Note that the pattern pieces are without seam allowance, so you will need to add the seam allowance after you draw the pattern on the fabric as required.

2 Working on the wrong side of your fabric, using your pattern pieces and allowing for a 1cm (⅜in) seam allowance, draw and cut out: from the flower-print cotton fabric (A), two body side pieces (one reversed), two bellies (one reversed), two head sides (one reversed), one head front, four leg bases, two ears (one reversed), two fore legs (one reversed), two hind legs (one reversed), one body back and a piece of fabric for the tail – draw two tails side by side on the fabric, then cut out as one rectangular piece remembering to allow for a 1cm (⅜in) seam allowance all around (note, the tail will be redrawn and cut to shape in step 8). Draw and cut out from the lilac cotton fabric (B), two ears (one reversed) and from the wadding (batting) (C), two ears. Cut two nostrils from the lilac felt (D) without seam allowance.

3 Place the belly pieces together with right sides facing, pin, then sew together along the long straight edge (3a). Open out the joined belly and place the legs on top so that right sides are facing, taking care to position the fore legs at the front of the belly and the hind legs at the back (3b). Pin, then sew in place around the curved edges.

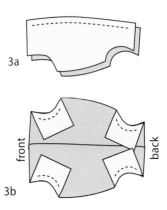

3a

3b

front / back

Cutting plan

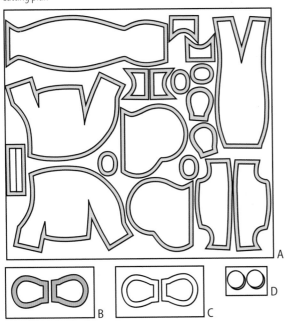

A

B

C

D

4 Now sew the darts on each body side piece (4a) (see Stitching Techniques) sewing the right-hand dart first (4b), then the left-hand dart (4c). Turn the body pieces over and admire from the front (4d).

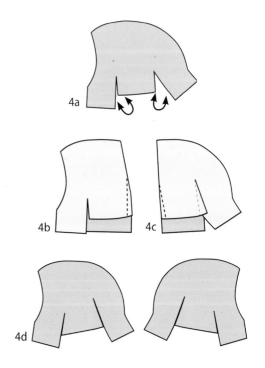

4a

4b

4c

4d

5 Now pin the body sides to the belly with right sides facing and sew up the sides of each leg and along the belly, leaving the leg ends open.

6 Place the leg base pieces at the ends of the hippo's short stumpy legs, with right sides facing (see diagram) and pin; sew together, first along one side, then along the other, to make the feet.

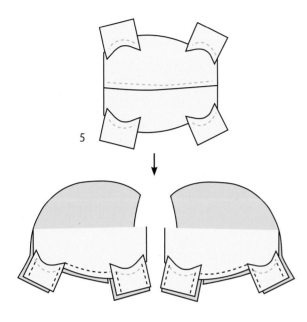

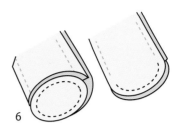

7 Fold the tail fabric in half with right sides facing and pin in place. Put the tail pattern on the fold and draw around its outline once more remembering to allow for a 1cm (⅜in) seam allowance – this way, you will only have to sew along one side of the tail. Starting at the folded edge, sew the tail leaving the end unstitched (7a). Trim the seam allowance (7b); turn the tail right side out and stuff with toy filling (7c).

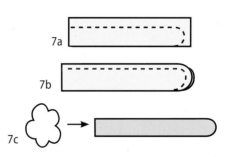

TIP: A chopstick comes in very useful when turning narrow pieces, such as Mary's tail, right side out (see Stitching Techniques).

8 Take the body back piece and fold it in half with right sides facing, placing the tail in between; sew the tail in position (see diagram).

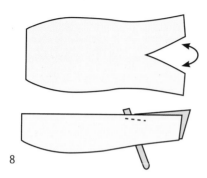

8

9 Place the body back and the body sides together with right sides facing, pin, then sew along each side of the back, from the neck to the bottom (9a and 9b); then pin and sew the bottom end of the body back onto the belly back side, just beneath the tail (9c) – there should be an opening between the seam just stitched and the tail for turning the hippo through later.

10 Referring to the markings on the pattern piece, sew the nostrils onto the right side of the head front.

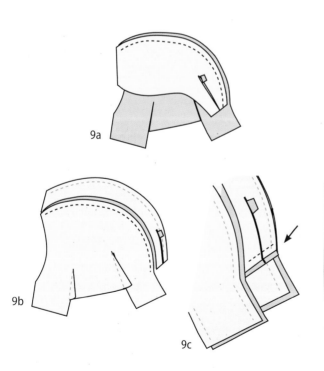

9a

9b

9c

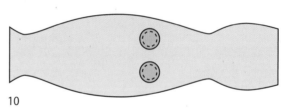

10

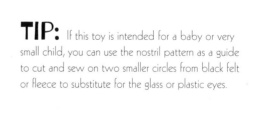

TIP: If this toy is intended for a baby or very small child, you can use the nostril pattern as a guide to cut and sew on two smaller circles from black felt or fleece to substitute for the glass or plastic eyes.

12 Pair up one lilac ear with one flower-print ear with right sides facing, then take a wadding (batting) ear and place underneath to sandwich the lilac ear in the middle. Pin and sew together leaving the straight edge unstitched. Trim the seam allowances and turn the ears right side out. Fold each ear in half at the bottom (unstitched) edge and sew together by hand.

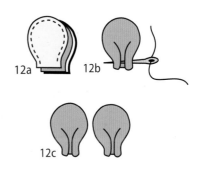

12a   12b

12c

TIP: If you do not have any wadding (batting) to hand, you can use a thick soft fabric to pad out the ears instead.

11 Take the head side pieces and fix the eyes in position as marked. Push the rod of the eye through the fabric from the right side, then, on the wrong side of the fabric, place the washer over the rod and push down until the washer rests against your work. If the rod won't go through the fabric, pierce the fabric first with the tip of a pair of scissors.

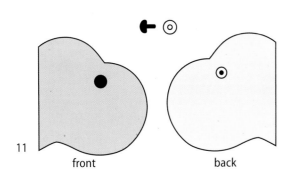

11

front   back

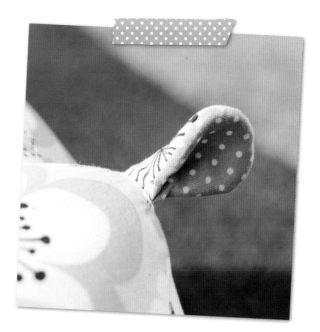

13 Take the head front piece and place the end marked top head along a head side piece with right sides facing, and position an ear in between; pin and sew together (13a). Now place the other head side on the other side of the head front with right sides facing; position an ear in between, pin and sew together (13b).

14 Now pin and sew the joined head onto the body joining the seams so that the right sides of the fabric are facing (see diagram).

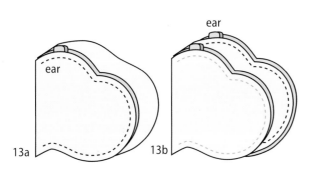

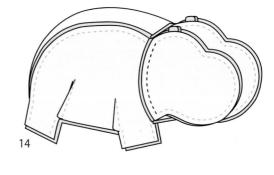

15 Turn the hippo right side out through the opening beneath the tail and fill with toy stuffing. Start with the nose and feet, then stuff the body. You will have to use a lot of toy filling to get a nice round shape. Once the stuffing is complete, hand sew the opening closed with ladder stitch (see Stitching Techniques).

TIP: It is particularly important to select a good quality toy filling to make Mary the hippo, as it is the stuffing that defines the round shape of her body. The toy filling you choose should be soft and bouncy, so disregard a stuffing if it is lumpy **before** you put it in your toy – it will be completely unsuitable. If you do see some lumps of toy filling on the outside of the hippo once she has been stuffed, you can use a chopstick to make a few adjustments to achieve a smooth finish.

15a

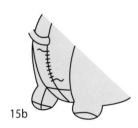

15b

Your hippo is finished!

TIP: If you want to customize the hippo, you can add a fun motif, such as a flower, or even a name to her back. Cut letters or shapes from fusible-web backed fabric, iron, then stitch in place. Refer to Stitching Techniques for more detailed instruction.

DARON THE DRAGON

With his fiery red belly, scaly backbone, pointed horns, vivid green wings and fire-breathing nostrils, Daron is a fearsome sight. Luckily, he is also a fearless protector of children, so he'll make a perfect bedtime companion for your child, who will be able to sleep safely and without fear because Daron the dragon is near! Get ready for some serious sewing with this pattern for the more experienced soft-toy maker.

You will need

Green cotton fabric for the body sides, head, upper wings, arms, legs, feet, outer nostrils and outer ears: 50 x 50cm (20 x 20in)

Red striped cotton fabric for the belly: 50 x 15cm (20 x 6in)

Red cotton fabric for the lower wings and inner ears: 25 x 25cm (10 x 10in)

Dark green cotton fabric for the inner nostrils: 10 x 5cm (4 x 2in)

White cotton fabric for the horns: 5 x 5cm (2 x 2in)

Black felt for the eyes: 5 x 5cm (2 x 2in)

Red felt for the spine: 45 x 5cm (18 x 2in)

Wadding (batting) for the wings: 25 x 20cm (10 x 8in)

Sewing thread

Toy filling

Steel ball filling or plastic pallet filling for tip of tail

Basic tool kit (see Tools & Techniques)

1 Make a copy of all the pattern pieces for Daron the dragon (see Patterns), remembering to transfer all the pattern markings too; cut out your pattern pieces. Join the pattern pieces for the body side, belly and spine. Note that the pattern pieces are without seam allowance, so you will need to add the seam allowance after you draw the pattern on the fabric as required.

2 Working on the wrong side of your fabric, using your pattern pieces and allowing for a 1cm (⅜in) seam allowance, draw and cut out: from the green cotton fabric (A), two body sides (one reversed), two wings (one reversed), two head sides (one reversed), two nostrils (one reversed), two ears (one reversed), two inside leg pieces (one reversed), two foot base pieces (one reversed), two upper foot pieces (one reversed), four arms (two reversed) and one head top; from the red striped cotton fabric (B), one belly; from the wadding (batting) (C), two wings; from the red cotton fabric (D), two ears (one reversed) and two wings (one reversed); and from the dark green cotton fabric (E), two nostrils (one reversed). Draw and cut out the following from the pieces of felt without seam allowance: from red felt (F), the spine; and from black felt (G), two eyes. (Note: the small piece of white cotton fabric will be used to make the horns in step 6.)

3 Pair up the arms with right sides facing, and pin in place. Sew the arms, leaving an opening for turning. Trim the seam allowances; turn the arms right side out and stuff with toy filling. Hand sew the opening closed with ladder stitch (see Stitching Techniques).

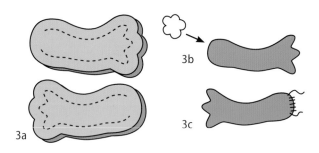

3a 3b 3c

TIP: A chopstick is the ideal tool to help you turn the arms right side out (see Stitching Techniques), and it will also come in useful for stuffing the tail in step 17.

Cutting plan

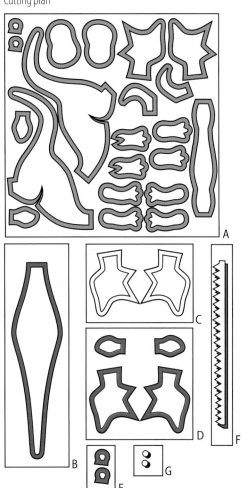

A
B
C
D
E
F
G

4 Pair up each green (outer) nostril piece with a dark (inner) green nostril piece with right sides facing and pin. Sew together leaving the straight edge unstitched (4a). Trim the seam allowances and turn the nostrils right side out (4b). Fold each nostril in half at the bottom (unstitched) edge and sew together by hand (4c).

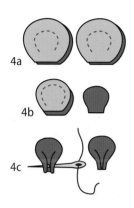

5 Pair up the red (inner) and green (outer) ear pieces with right sides facing. Pin, then sew together leaving the straight edge unstitched. Trim the seam allowances and turn the ears right side out. Fold each ear in half at the bottom (unstitched) edge and sew together by hand.

6 Now make the horns. Take the small piece of white cotton fabric: cut it in half and pin together with right sides facing. Use the horn pattern to draw two horns onto the pinned fabric (6a). Sew around the marked outlines leaving the straight edges unstitched (6b). Cut the horns out close to the stitching line, and turn right side out (6c).

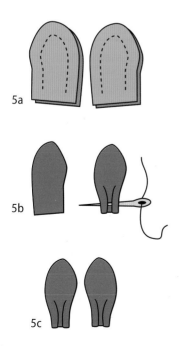

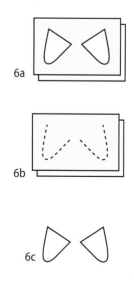

7 Pair up one red wing with one green wing with right sides facing, then take a wadding (batting) wing, place underneath and pin through the layers. Sew together leaving the straight edge unstitched (7a). Trim the seam allowances and turn the wings right side out. Sew the lines marked on the wing pattern (7b). Hand sew the opening closed with ladder stitch.

8 Sew the felt eyes onto the right side of the head side pieces (8a – see pattern for placement). Pin the head top around one of the head side pieces with right sides facing, taking care to join up the points marked A and B on the pattern, and placing a horn and a nostril in between the two layers following the pattern markings. Sew together, starting from the back. Repeat to join the other head side to the head top (8b). Trim the seam allowances; turn the head right side out and stuff with toy filling (8c).

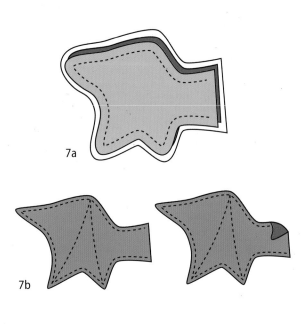

7a

7b

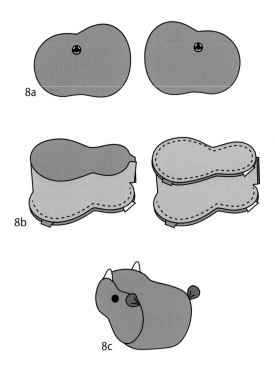

8a

8b

8c

TIP: The addition of a wadding (batting) layer will make the wing stronger; if you don't have any wadding (batting), use one or two layers of thick fabric or fleece instead.

9 Put the ears in the turning gap and hand sew the opening closed with ladder stitch.

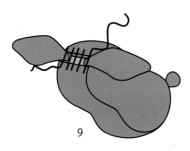

9

12 The joining on of the upper feet is the most difficult step in sewing the dragon. Take a good look at the diagram and work carefully. Now you sew part of the upper foot onto the leg: join 'A' marked on the upper foot to 'A upper foot' as marked on the body side, and the side marked 'B' on the upper foot to 'B upper foot' as marked on the inside leg. Now sew together the parts marked 'C inside leg' on the body side and 'C body side' on the inside leg, again with right sides facing.

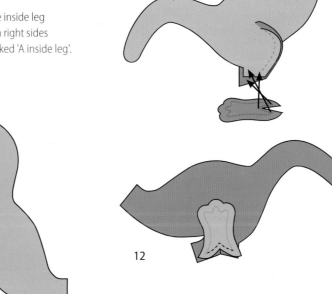

12

10 Now to make up the body. Place one of the inside leg pieces on top of one of the body sides with right sides facing. Pin, then sew together along the side marked 'A inside leg'.

10

11 Now you need to sew sides B onto each other with right sides facing. This is a difficult step and you should fold back the fabric as shown on the diagram to make this easier.

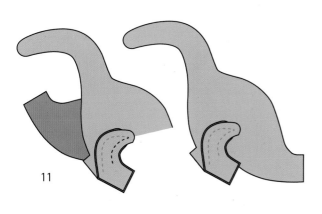

11

13 Repeat steps 10, 11 and 12 to join the remaining body side, inside leg and upper foot pieces.

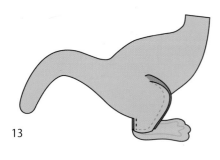

13

15 Place the spiky red felt spine in between the two body sides, with right sides facing so that the points of the spikes are facing inwards; pin and stitch in place.

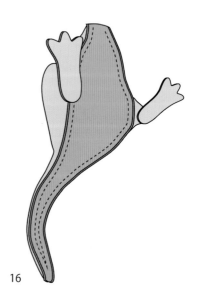

15

14 Before joining the two sides of the dragon's body, you must first sew the foot base onto the upper foot/leg on each side of the body. Pin, then sew them on with right sides facing.

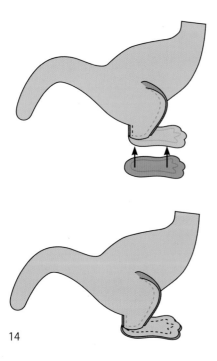

14

16 Pin, then sew the belly onto the body joining up points A, B, C and D marked on the body sides with points A, B, C and D marked on the belly.

16

17 Stuff the dragon's body with toy filling, starting with the tail taking small pieces and pushing them in with a chopstick.

18 Hand sew the head, the arms and the wings onto the body (see pattern for correct positioning) using ladder stitch.

17

18

TIP: Putting some heavier stuffing, such as steel ball filling or plastic pallet filling, in the tip of the tail is highly recommended as the heavier the tail tip is, the better the dragon will stand when it is finished.

Your dragon is done!

TOOLS & TECHNIQUES

BASIC TOOL KIT

To make the toys in this book you need some essential tools and equipment, and everything that you will require is described here.

Sewing machine

Although you can sew all the toys included in this book by hand, a sewing machine will certainly help speed up the process, and the finished toy will look more professional. However, a basic sewing machine – one with a straight and zigzag stitch – is all you need. A speed setting control, which allows you to slow the sewing speed down, comes in very handy when sewing small toy parts, but although nice to have, this is not essential. An open-toe sewing machine foot is really useful when making soft toys – you can see the pattern lines more clearly and it really helps when sewing on parts such as eyes and mouths.

Dressmaker's pins

Generally it is a good idea to pin fabric pieces together before sewing to keep them in position, so invest in some good quality anti-rust pins. For more on pinning, see Stitching Techniques.

TIP: Always remove pins as you sew and never sew over them, as you will risk damaging your sewing needle, or even your machine.

Chopstick

A chopstick makes a great tool for stuffing. It is particularly useful for getting toy filling into the hard to reach places, or for smoothing out lumpy stuffing (see Stuffing Techniques). I recommend using a plastic chopstick, as the wooden sticks can be too sharp. Plastic chopsticks tend to be rounder, have a smoother surface and are very durable.

Sewing thread

You should always use a good quality polyester sewing thread when sewing toys to ensure strong seams that can withstand boisterous play sessions – you don't want the toys falling apart when they are being played with.

Embroidery thread (floss) and dollmaker's needle

You will need six-strand embroidery thread (floss) for sewing details such as the claws onto Tyler the tiger and Brody the dog. A dollmaker's needle (which is an extra-long needle) will come in useful for this.

Pencil/fabric markers

There are many kinds of fabric markers available, but I just use a normal pencil or a regular marker to draw out the patterns. However, if you want to be absolutely sure that the pattern markings are not permanently visible on your fabric, you may prefer to use a vanishing marker. For more information on drawing patterns and transferring pattern markings, see Patterns.

Toy filling

There are different kinds of toy filling available. I recommend that you buy a high-quality toy filling that has lots of bounce to it. This will give your toy a nice look, and the toy will be very soft and therefore very huggable. If you buy a lower quality toy filling, you run the risk that lumps will form in your toy, with harder and softer parts. Try out a variety of fillings to see what works best for you. When you want a part of your toy to be a bit heavier (such as the tail or legs) you can use steel ball filling or plastic pellet filling.

Iron and ironing board

Iron your fabric first before drawing the pattern onto it to get rid of any creases. An iron is also required when using fusible webbing.

Hand sewing needles

You'll need these to close up the turning gaps and for hand sewing body parts onto some of the toys.

Scissors

You need a sharp pair of fabric scissors for cutting out fabric and a separate pair of paper scissors to cut out the paper patterns. But don't mix them up – cutting paper with your fabric scissors will blunt them. There are many types of fabric scissors available – choose a pair that feels comfortable in your hand.

Craft knife

This may come in useful when cutting faux fur fabrics (see Fabrics).

The addition of a little heavier filling such as steel ball filling to the end of the dragon's tail helps to keep him standing upright.

Fusible webbing

This is a double-sided adhesive paper used for fabric appliqué, such as the patches on Brody the dog and the fringe (bangs) on Emilio. When you iron it onto a fabric it sticks permanently, so that the fabric will not fray; then the backing is removed from the fusible webbing and the appliqué patch can be ironed into place on your toy for a permanent fixing. The appliqué can be stitched to give it a hand-sewn look, but this is not strictly necessary (see Stitching Techniques for more information on how to use fusible webbing).

FABRICS

Fabric shopping is a part of the fun of making a new toy. There are so many colours and designs available, and while my designs can provide you with ideas, remember that you can make your toy just the way you want it, in any colour you choose.

Cotton

Almost every toy in this book is made from 100% cotton, which is readily available online and in fabric shops or even at your local market, but you can use any fabric you like. The most important thing is to choose good quality fabrics to ensure long-lasting toys.

By picking out your own fabrics you can make your toy a very personal design. If you have trouble choosing between all the wonderful fabrics available, why not make more than one version?

Fleece

Fleece is perfect for soft-toy making as it is so soft. It is a very forgiving fabric and an uneven stitching line will hardly be noticeable once the fabric is turned through to the right side. If you are a beginner sewer and you find cotton hard to work with, I recommend practising with fleece first. When you are more comfortable with your sewing machine, you can try making the toys again using cotton fabric.

This duo is a great example of how important fabric choice can be. For Emma, I chose a pretty graphic flower print fabric for her dress, and a miniature polka dot for her tights and shoes. The fabric chosen for her hair makes it look as if she has curls galore. For Emilio, I chose a small-scale print for his T-shirt, and I was especially pleased with the diamond trellis print I found for his shoes.

Felt

For the smallest parts on my toys, such as facial details for example, I generally use felt. It is easy to cut, it doesn't fray and it keeps its shape well, making even the tiniest pieces easy to sew on. It is available in so many colours, but there is just one small problem – felt can't be washed in a washing machine, so you will need to clean the toys by hand. If you want machine-washable toys, substitute fleece for felt. Alternatively, you could use cotton, applying the pieces with fusible webbing (see Stitching Techniques).

Faux fur

Faux fur is a good fabric to use for soft toys as it makes them look even more huggable. It is available in many colours and fur lengths: it does make a mess when cut, so keep your vacuum cleaner nearby. To cut faux fur, use small scissors with short blades; lift the fabric slightly and insert the scissors just under the woven backing, but take care not to cut through the fur pile on the front of the fabric. Alternatively, you could use a craft knife to cut out your pieces, but don't cut too deep: cut through the backing only, not the fur.

By using felt you can add lots of detail to your soft toys so easily. Several layers of felt are used to make Wooksy the owl's sleepy eyes.

Gronk the monster is one very huggable toy thanks to his very soft, faux fur body.

Fleece works really well for the many stripes of Tyler the tiger. It doesn't fray and it is very soft, making him very easy to cuddle.

Other fabrics

There are many other fabrics you can use to make these soft-toy patterns: you might even want to recycle some family garments as a lasting memory – you could use one of daddy's worn-out shirts or baby's outgrown clothes. There are, however, a couple of things to keep in mind when choosing fabrics. If a fabric is very stretchy, the shape of the toy will be different. If, for example, you are sewing a doll and the fabric stretches horizontally, your doll will become wider, and if the fabric stretches vertically, it will become taller. Stiff fabrics such as denim are very difficult to work with, so these may not be suitable. If you are unsure about a fabric, try using it to make a small part of the toy first, such as an ear or an arm; if that works well, you can use it for the rest of the toy too.

STITCHING TECHNIQUES

The stitching techniques used to create the toys are explained in detail here, from pinning your fabric prior to stitching, to hand and machine sewing advice, as well as a guide to using fusible webbing. Follow this advice to create your quality toys.

Pinning

Pins are very useful tools to keep fabric pieces together when sewing. Pin through the pattern lines that you have drawn onto the fabric to make sure the pieces are placed exactly on top of each other. If you place two fabric pieces with the right sides together, first pin through the pattern line on the top piece and then through the pattern line of the bottom piece.

Hand sewing

BACKSTITCH

A backstitch looks like a regular machine stitch, creating a continuous line of stitching. Work even, small stitches following the diagram.

Pin fabric pieces together before sewing: never machine stitch over pins but remove them as you go to avoid damaging your sewing machine.

Brody's nose is sewn on with a neat backstitch worked by hand, but his eye patch has been embroidered with a machine zigzag stitch.

LADDER STITCH

This is an invisible stitch used to close openings and to sew parts onto your toy.

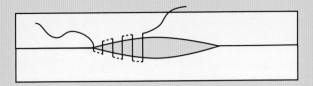

Using ladder stitch to close a turning gap: start by sewing ladder stitch over one of the stitched sides next to the gap, working several stitches until the thread is secured, then continue across the hole to close the gap. When you reach the other stitched side, continue to ladder stitch a little way to secure the thread.

Using ladder stitch to sew a tail (or other small body part) onto a toy: first sew a few small stitches where the part will be placed to secure the thread, then ladder stitch the tail in place as shown. Once the part is stitched on, sew a few small stitches beneath it to secure the thread. Pull the thread to check that it is secured before finishing off.

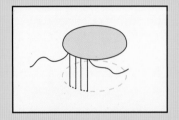

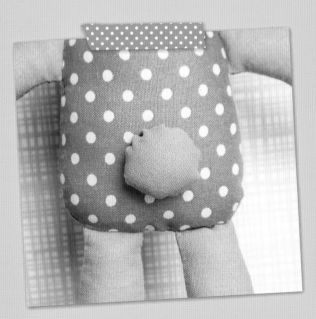

When using ladder stitch to sew on a body part, such as a tail, secure the thread on a spot where the part will be placed so it will be hidden.

Machine sewing

STRAIGHT STITCH

When sewing your toys, use the standard size straight stitch on your machine, which is usually 2.5mm (³⁄₃₂in). When beginning to machine stitch, secure your stitching by starting and ending with a few reverse stitches.

ZIGZAG STITCH

To create a nice embroidery effect on your toys, I recommend using the following setting for the zigzag stitch: width 4.0mm; length 0.5–0.8mm. Settings may vary depending on your sewing machine, try out the zigzag stitch on a piece of test fabric first and make any necessary adjustments to the setting before stitching onto your toy.

STITCHING A DART

Several of the projects require darts to be sewn, Tyler the tiger and Brody the dog for example. In the diagram, you can see how you should cut out the fabric around the dart (A), and how to fold the fabric prior to stitching, pinning it in place (B). To sew the dart (C), start at the bottom of the pattern line and sew towards the point. Sew off the fabric, and knot the thread but don't pull too hard – if you do a wrinkle will form on the point of the dart. Open the fabric and your dart is done (D); turn it over and admire it from the front (E).

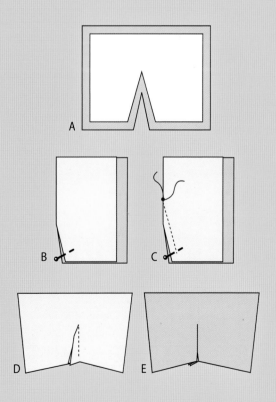

How to use fusible webbing

Iron the fusible webbing onto the wrong side of your appliqué fabric and allow to cool (A). Pull off the protective layer from the fusible webbing (B) and draw around your pattern piece onto the fusible-web backed fabric (C). Unless indicated otherwise, cut out the marked shape without seam allowance (D). Now place the fabric piece, fusible-web side down onto, the right side of the fabric it is to be appliquéd to and iron in place (E).

The fusible webbing will stick the fabric pieces together permanently and the fabric will not fray, but stitching around the appliqué gives a nice decorative finish (F). You could use a standard straight machine stitch, but I prefer a zigzag stitch because it gives a more professional look. It is very easy to do. Set your machine to the zigzag stitch and set the stitch width to very small. The smaller the zigzag width, the more embroidered it will look. Test stitch first on a piece of scrap fabric to check the effect.

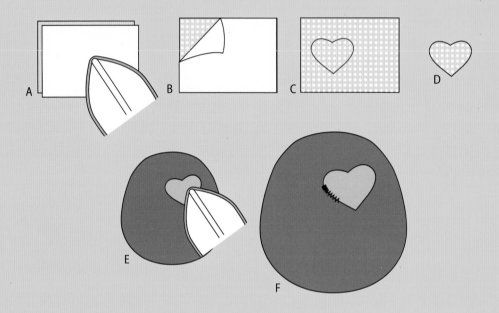

Turning narrow, long pieces

Turning narrow, long body pieces, such as arms, legs and tails, right side out once they are stitched can be very time consuming, but there is a trick to make this a little easier. Take a long stick – a chopstick is ideal – and put it at the stitched end of the sewn part. Now push the fabric over the stick with your hand.

TIP: Stuffing narrow, long pieces is also a little tricky but a chopstick will make the task a bit easier: put small pieces of stuffing in the opening and push them in with the chopstick.

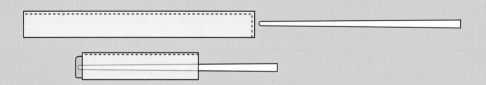

STUFFING TECHNIQUES

You are almost finished, but a well-stitched toy needs a good stuffing! Read the following advice to help you turn your sewn project into a well-stuffed plush.

Tools and tips

Stuffing your toy is a very important step in toy making and choosing a good toy filling is essential (see Basic Tool Kit). If your toy doesn't have enough toy filling in it, the shape will not look as good as a well-stuffed plush.

For the most part, you will be stuffing the toy filling using your hands. If when you have stuffed your toy, you find you need to rearrange some of the filling for a smoother finish, you don't have to pull it all out again. A chopstick can be used to gently manipulate the toy filling into a more consistent shape. Alternatively, use the handle of a paintbrush but just make sure it is not too thin as you don't want it to make holes in your fabric.

When stuffing a toy with small, attached open parts, like the hippo's feet, start by putting toy filling in the feet (or other small parts) until they are strong and sturdy, then fill the body with big lumps of toy filling.

95

PATTERNS

Working with the patterns

Make a photocopy of the pattern you are going to use, or trace the pattern pieces onto thin paper or tracing paper. Remember to transfer all the pattern markings too. Some patterns are divided into two parts and these need to be joined to create one pattern piece. Copy both pattern pieces, making sure to copy the joining circles marked on these pattern pieces too. To join the two into one pattern piece, overlap them to align the joining circles: it helps to put the parts against a window so you can see through the paper. Once the pattern pieces are in alignment, use tape to stick them together.

Drawing the patterns onto fabric

Lay your fabric on a flat surface, such as a table or floor. Put the pattern on the wrong side of the fabric, put something heavy on it to make sure it stays in place, then use a 4B or 6B pencil or a fabric marker pen to draw around the edge of the pattern piece, as close as you can get. Remember to add a 1cm (⅜in) seam allowance, but this doesn't have to be very precise: use the drawn pattern lines as your guideline. When you are using fleece, use a marker to draw out pattern pieces onto the fabric, and pick a colour that is close to the fabric colour.

Don't forget to transfer the pattern markings to the fabric those that are at the side of the pattern (leg and ear placements, for example) can be marked on the seam allowance of the fabric. To place details, such as eyes or mouths, in the correct position, cut out the detail from the paper pattern, line up the pattern onto the fabric once more, and use the cut out detail as a stencil to transfer the marking.

Making your own tracing paper

Tracing paper is something that you can easily create yourself. All you need are regular 75g paper (printer paper), vegetable oil and a paintbrush. Paint the paper with the vegetable oil and let it dry. (I recommend placing the paper on newspaper before painting it with oil as it does leave a bit of a mess.)

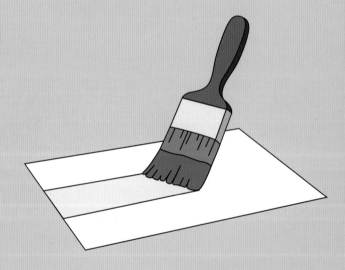

TIP: As all the patterns are reproduced full size, you can copy or trace them and start work immediately as no resizing is required.

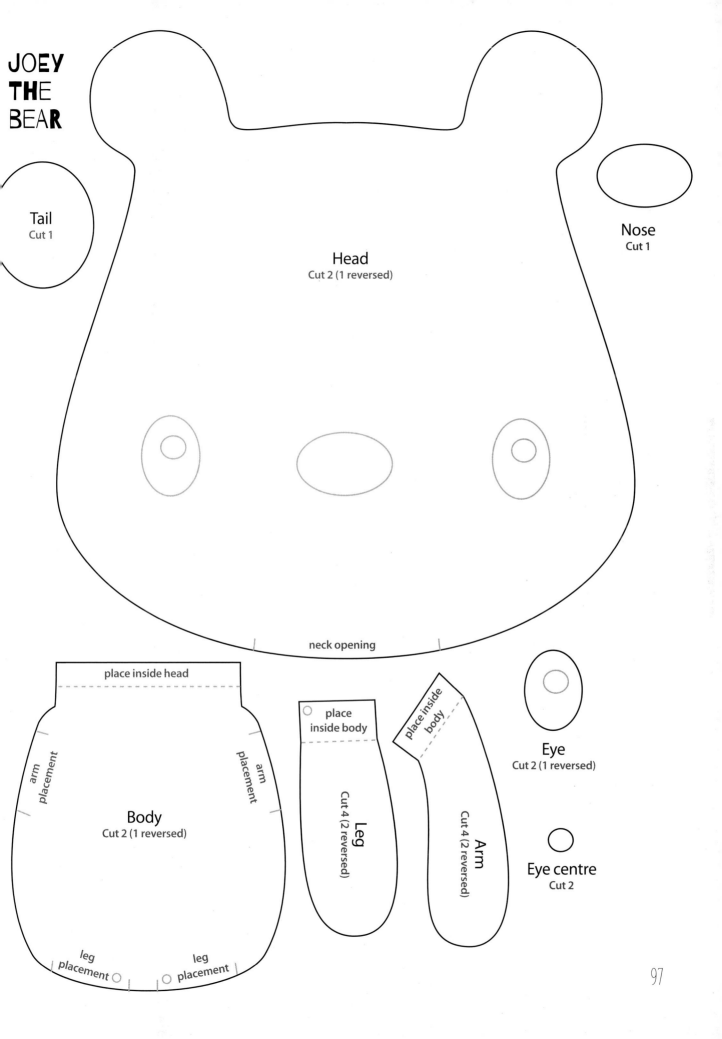

JOEY
THE
BEAR

Tail
Cut 1

Head
Cut 2 (1 reversed)

Nose
Cut 1

neck opening

place inside head

arm placement

arm placement

Body
Cut 2 (1 reversed)

leg placement

leg placement

place inside body

Leg
Cut 4 (2 reversed)

place inside body

Arm
Cut 4 (2 reversed)

Eye
Cut 2 (1 reversed)

Eye centre
Cut 2

97

WOOKSY THE OWL

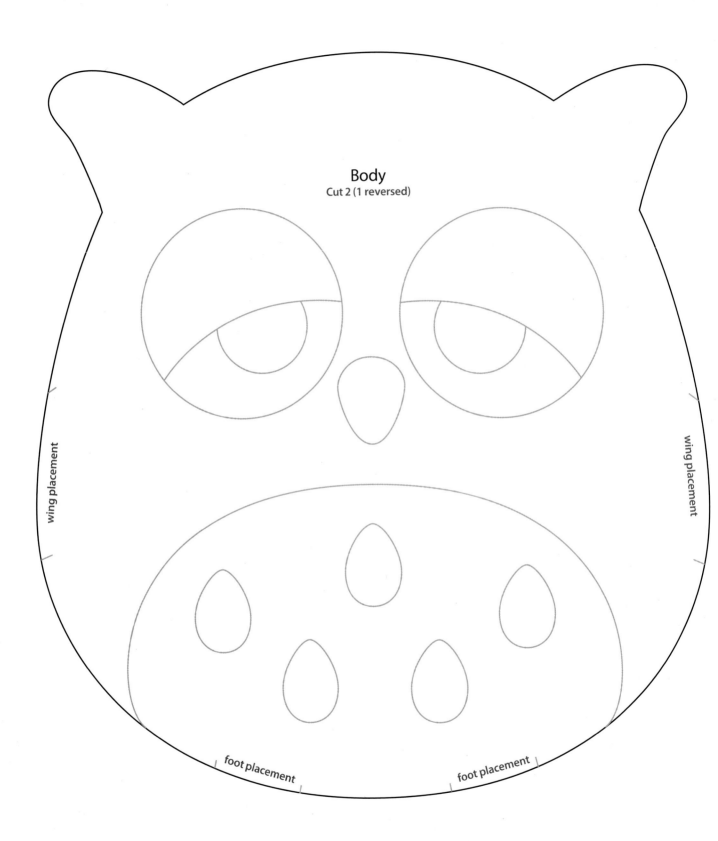

Body
Cut 2 (1 reversed)

wing placement

wing placement

foot placement

foot placement

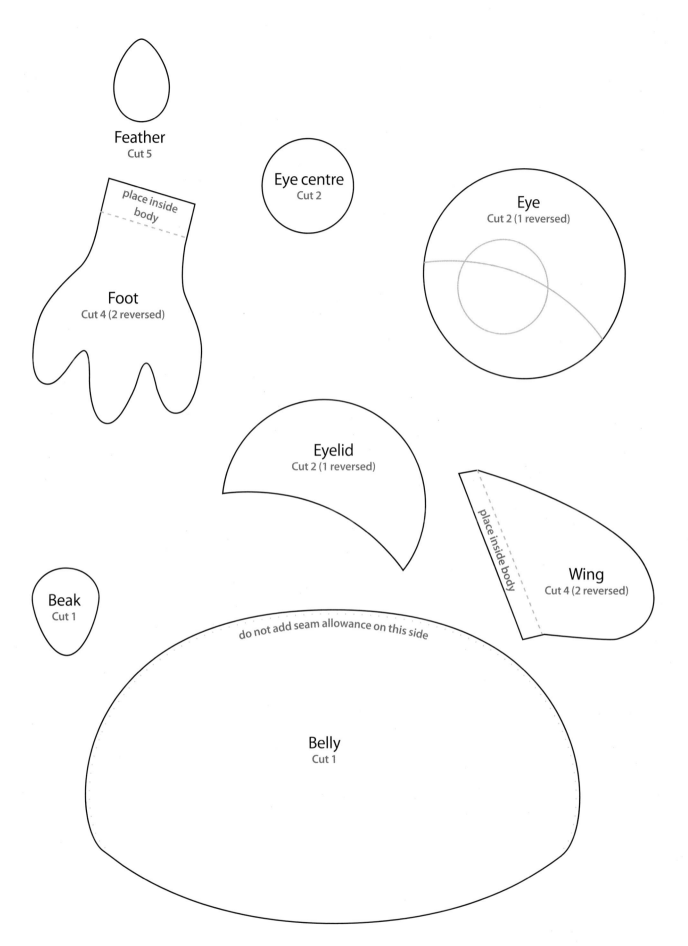

Feather
Cut 5

Eye centre
Cut 2

Eye
Cut 2 (1 reversed)

place inside body

Foot
Cut 4 (2 reversed)

Eyelid
Cut 2 (1 reversed)

place inside body

Wing
Cut 4 (2 reversed)

Beak
Cut 1

do not add seam allowance on this side

Belly
Cut 1

MISSY THE KOALA

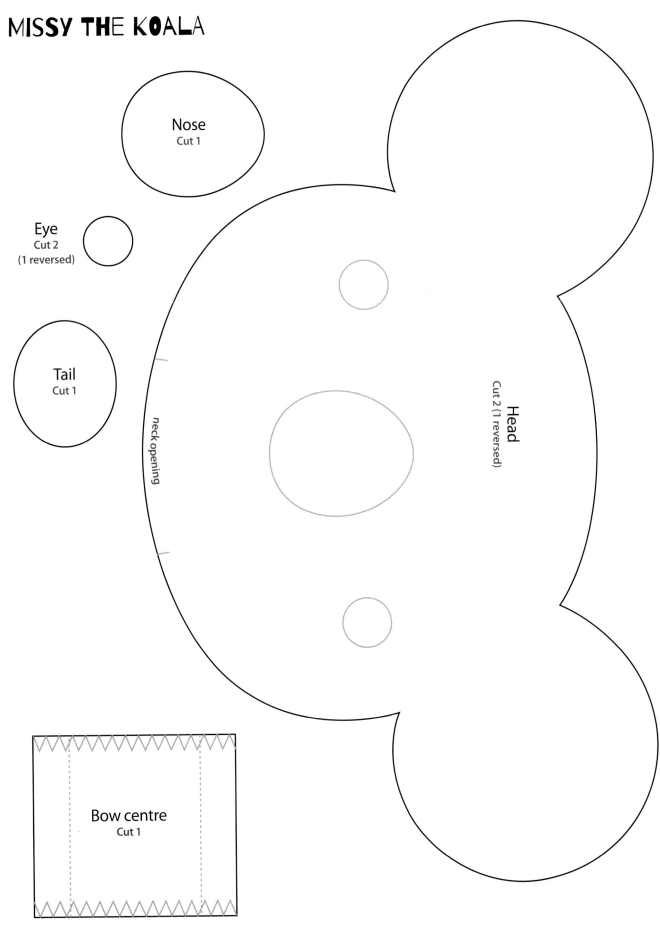

Nose
Cut 1

Eye
Cut 2
(1 reversed)

Tail
Cut 1

neck opening

Head
Cut 2 (1 reversed)

Bow centre
Cut 1

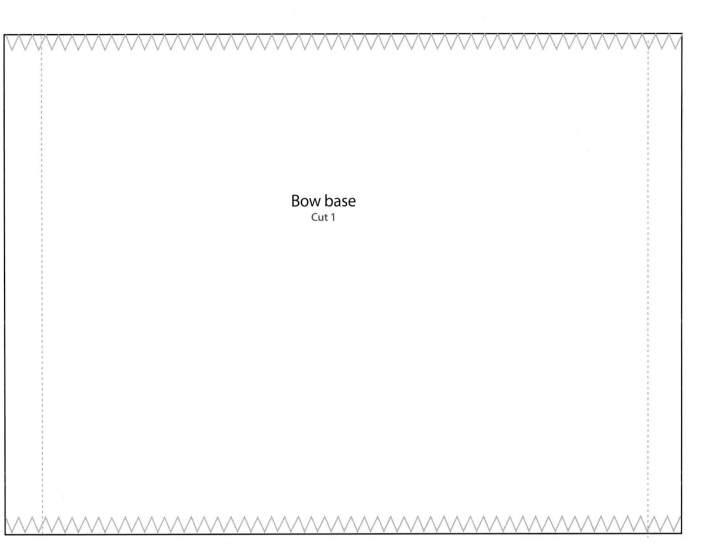

Bow base
Cut 1

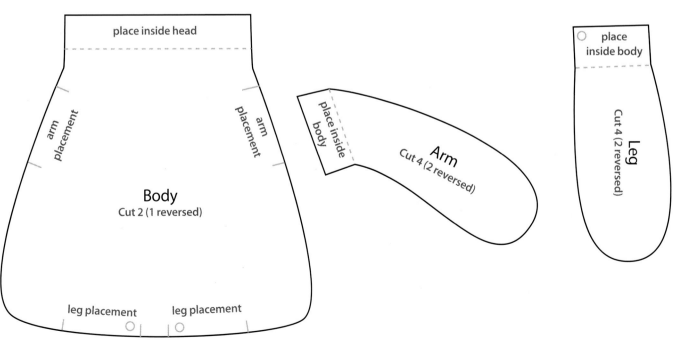

place inside head

arm placement

arm placement

Body
Cut 2 (1 reversed)

leg placement

leg placement

place inside body

Arm
Cut 4 (2 reversed)

place inside body

Leg
Cut 4 (2 reversed)

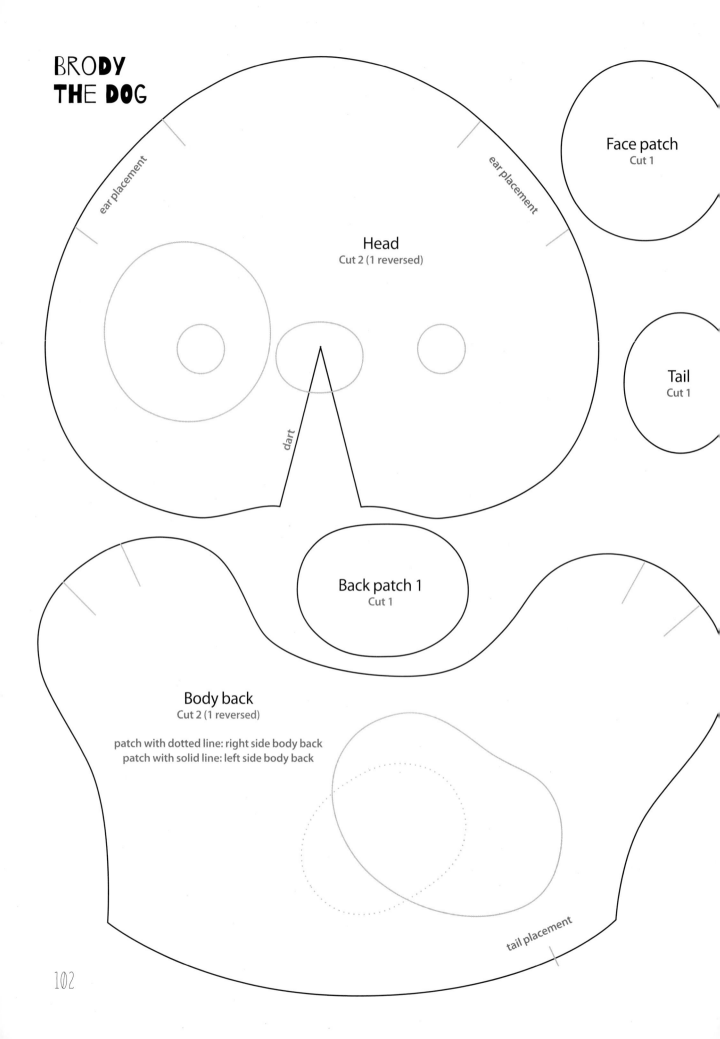

BRODY
THE DOG

Face patch
Cut 1

Head
Cut 2 (1 reversed)

ear placement

ear placement

dart

Tail
Cut 1

Back patch 1
Cut 1

Body back
Cut 2 (1 reversed)

patch with dotted line: right side body back
patch with solid line: left side body back

tail placement

102

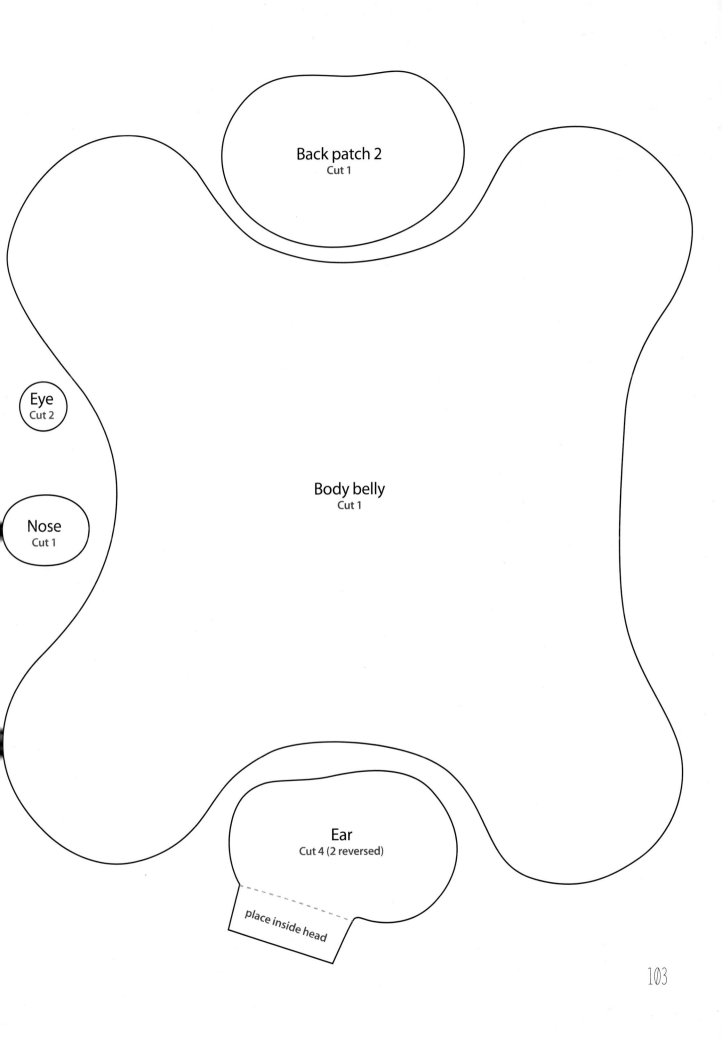

Back patch 2
Cut 1

Eye
Cut 2

Body belly
Cut 1

Nose
Cut 1

Ear
Cut 4 (2 reversed)

place inside head

KITTY THE CAT

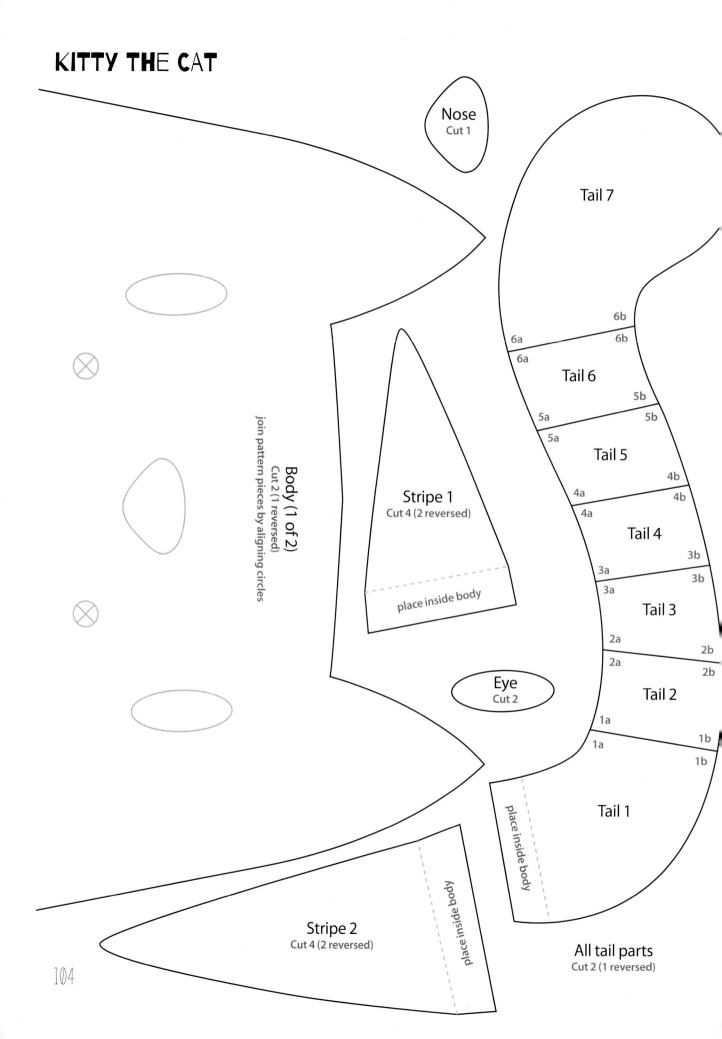

Nose
Cut 1

Tail 7

6b
6a
6a
6b
6a

Tail 6

5b
5a
5b
5a

Tail 5

4b
4a
4b
4a

Tail 4

3b
3a
3b
3a

Tail 3

2a
2b
2a
2b

Tail 2

1a
1a
1b
1b

Tail 1

place inside body

Body (1 of 2)
Cut 2 (1 reversed)
join pattern pieces by aligning circles

Stripe 1
Cut 4 (2 reversed)

place inside body

Eye
Cut 2

Stripe 2
Cut 4 (2 reversed)

place inside body

All tail parts
Cut 2 (1 reversed)

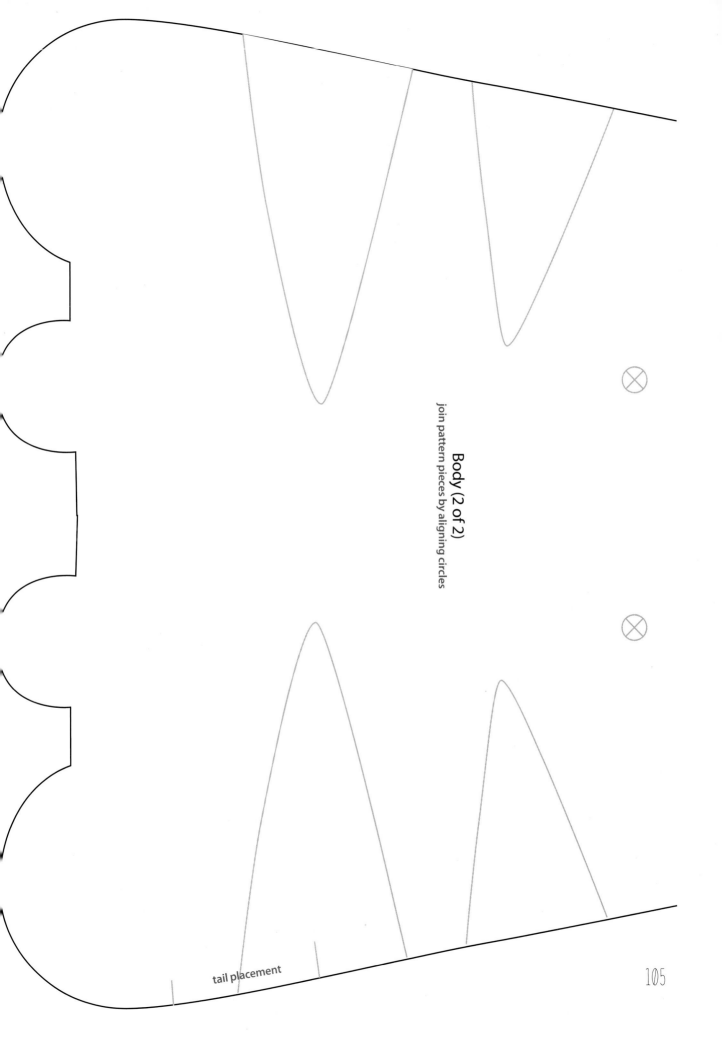

Body (2 of 2)
join pattern pieces by aligning circles

tail placement

EMMA THE GIRL

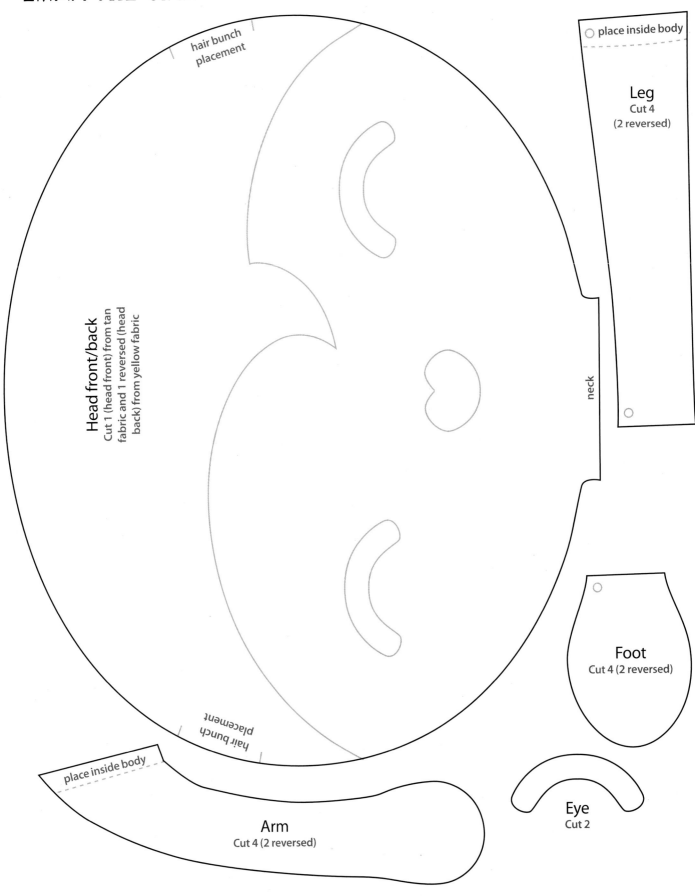

hair bunch placement

Head front/back
Cut 1 (head front) from tan fabric and 1 reversed (head back) from yellow fabric

hair bunch placement

neck

place inside body

Leg
Cut 4
(2 reversed)

Foot
Cut 4 (2 reversed)

place inside body

Arm
Cut 4 (2 reversed)

Eye
Cut 2

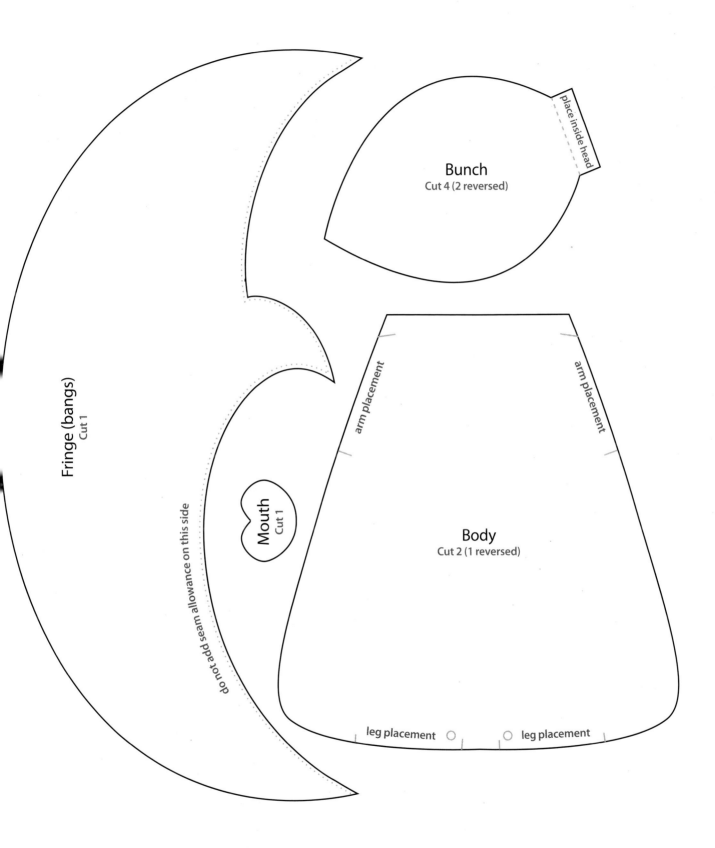

Bunch
Cut 4 (2 reversed)

place inside head

Fringe (bangs)
Cut 1

do not add seam allowance on this side

Mouth
Cut 1

arm placement

arm placement

Body
Cut 2 (1 reversed)

leg placement ○   ○ leg placement

EMILIO THE BOY

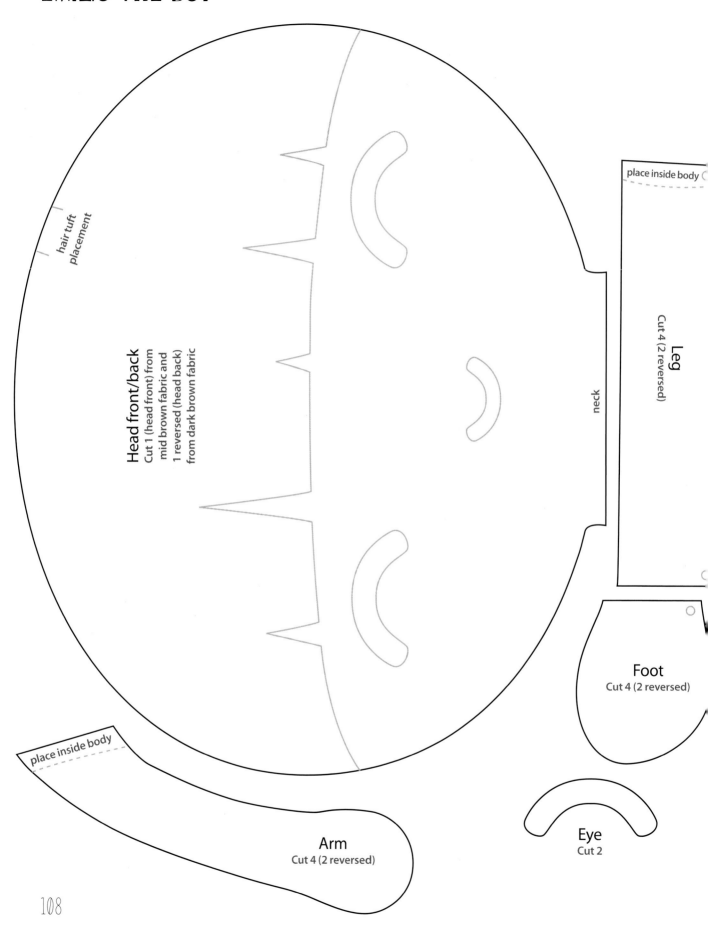

hair tuft placement

Head front/back
Cut 1 (head front) from
mid brown fabric and
1 reversed (head back)
from dark brown fabric

neck

place inside body

Leg
Cut 4 (2 reversed)

Foot
Cut 4 (2 reversed)

place inside body

Arm
Cut 4 (2 reversed)

Eye
Cut 2

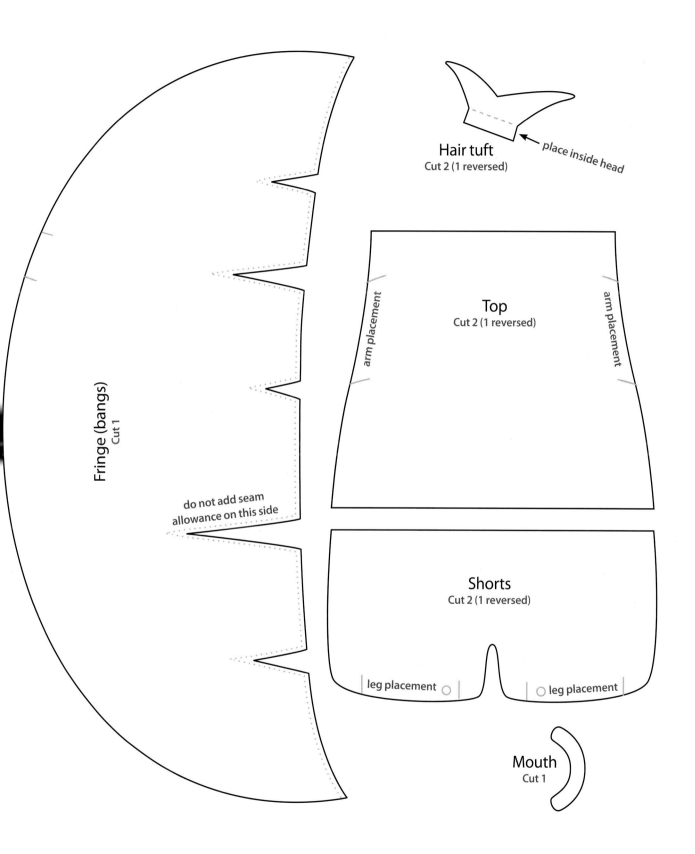

Fringe (bangs)
Cut 1

do not add seam
allowance on this side

Hair tuft
Cut 2 (1 reversed)

place inside head

Top
Cut 2 (1 reversed)

arm placement

arm placement

Shorts
Cut 2 (1 reversed)

leg placement ○

○ leg placement

Mouth
Cut 1

GRONK THE MONSTER

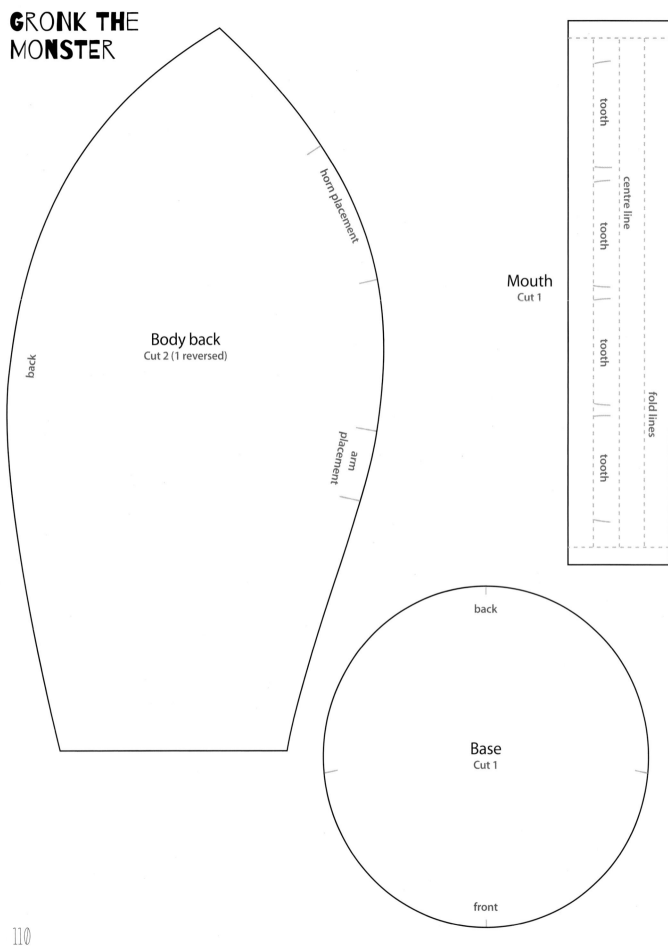

Body back
Cut 2 (1 reversed)

back

horn placement

arm placement

Mouth
Cut 1

tooth

tooth

tooth

tooth

tooth

centre line

fold lines

Base
Cut 1

back

front

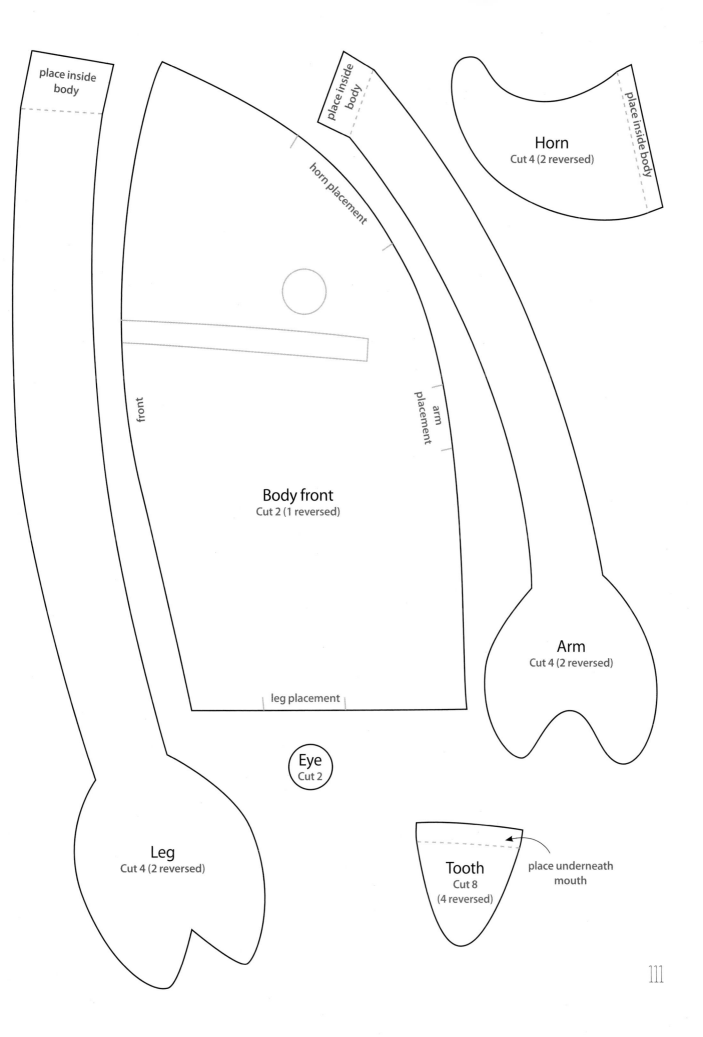

place inside body

place inside body

Horn
Cut 4 (2 reversed)

place inside body

horn placement

front

arm placement

Body front
Cut 2 (1 reversed)

Arm
Cut 4 (2 reversed)

leg placement

Eye
Cut 2

Leg
Cut 4 (2 reversed)

Tooth
Cut 8
(4 reversed)

place underneath mouth

111

PATRICK THE MONKEY

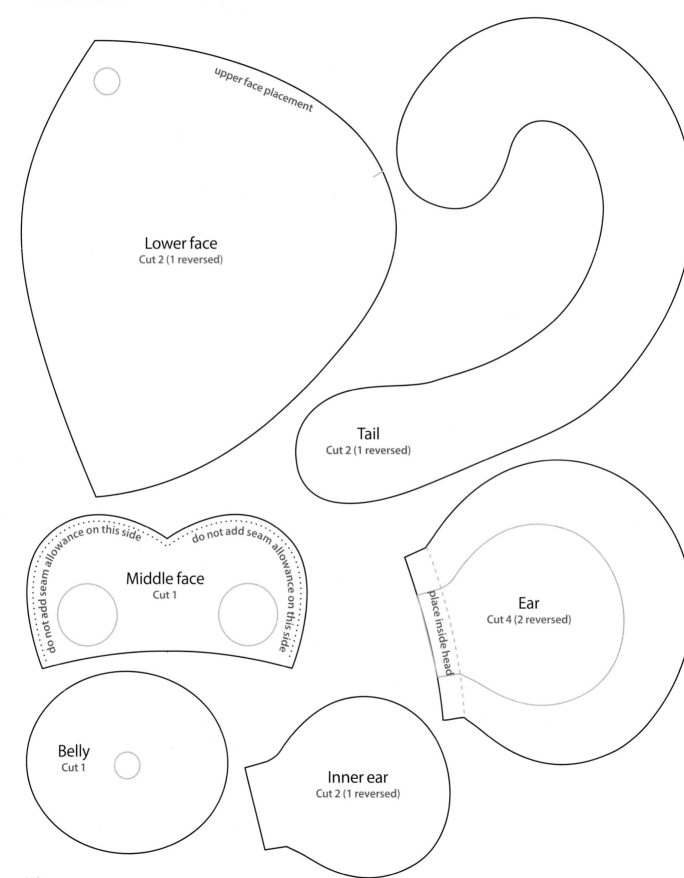

upper face placement

Lower face
Cut 2 (1 reversed)

Tail
Cut 2 (1 reversed)

do not add seam allowance on this side

do not add seam allowance on this side

Middle face
Cut 1

Ear
Cut 4 (2 reversed)

place inside head

Belly
Cut 1

Inner ear
Cut 2 (1 reversed)

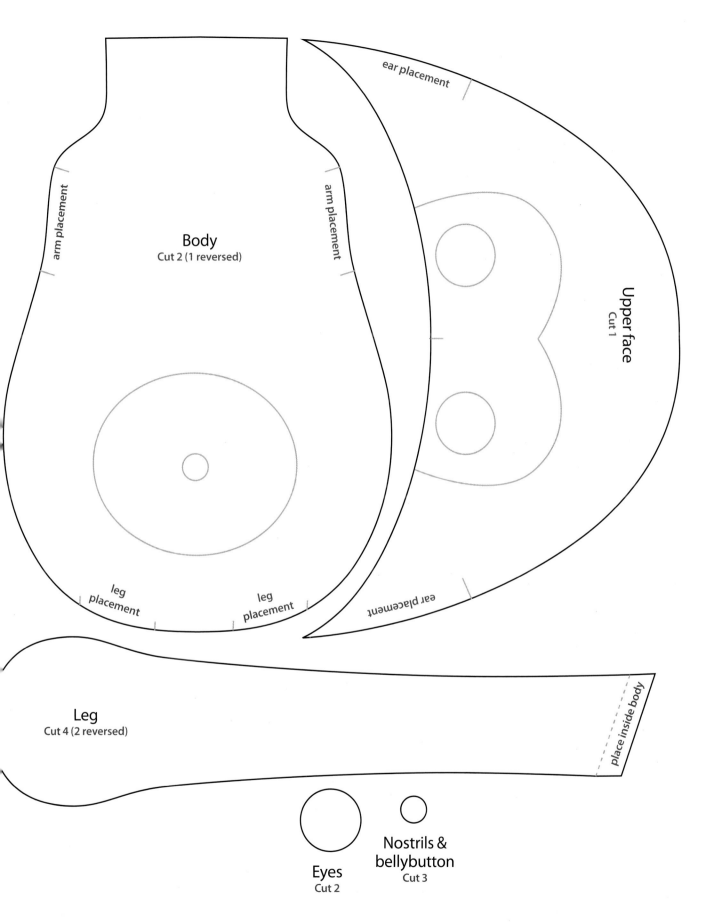

Body
Cut 2 (1 reversed)

arm placement

arm placement

leg placement

leg placement

ear placement

Upper face
Cut 1

ear placement

place inside body

Leg
Cut 4 (2 reversed)

Eyes
Cut 2

Nostrils &
bellybutton
Cut 3

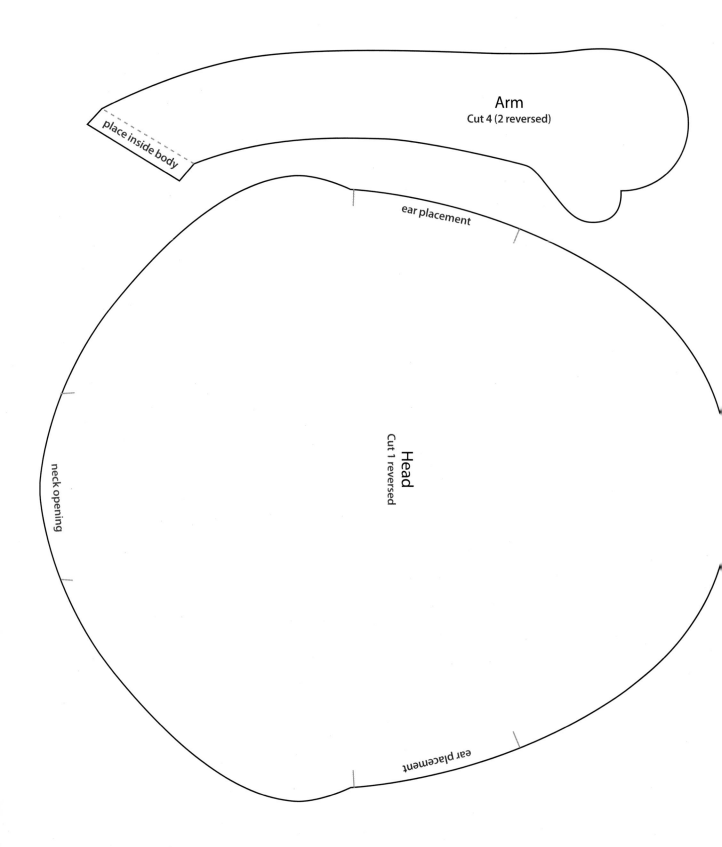

Arm
Cut 4 (2 reversed)

place inside body

ear placement

Head
Cut 1 reversed

neck opening

ear placement

ear placement

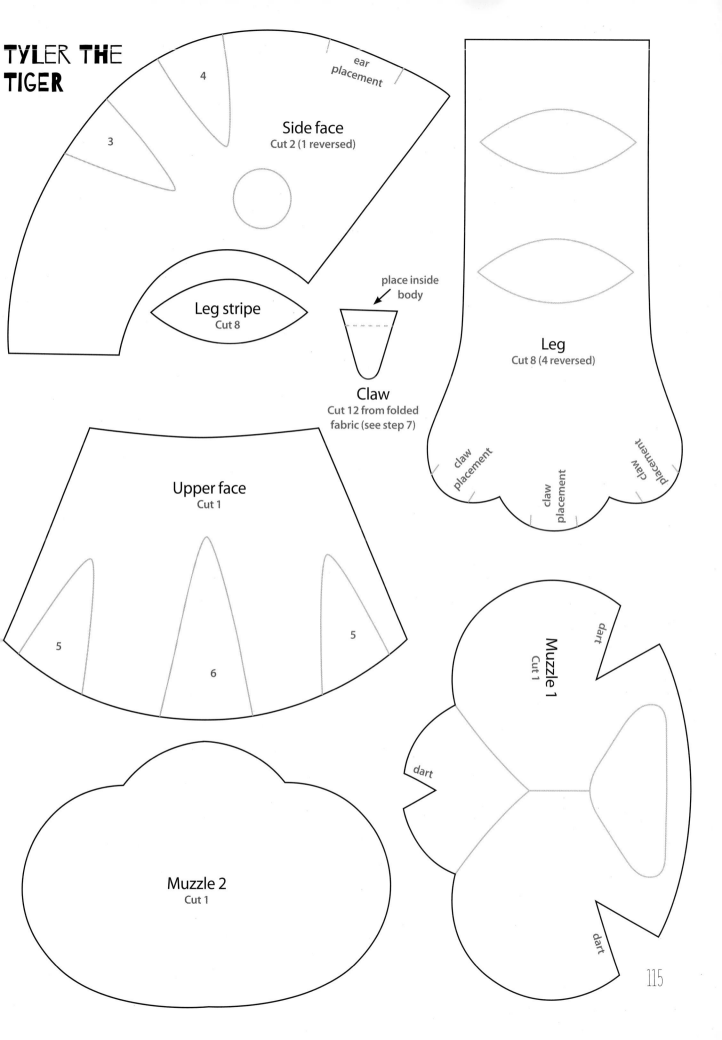

TYLER THE TIGER

Side face
Cut 2 (1 reversed)

ear placement

4

3

Leg stripe
Cut 8

place inside body

Claw
Cut 12 from folded fabric (see step 7)

Leg
Cut 8 (4 reversed)

claw placement

claw placement

claw placement

Upper face
Cut 1

5

6

5

Muzzle 1
Cut 1

dart

dart

dart

Muzzle 2
Cut 1

115

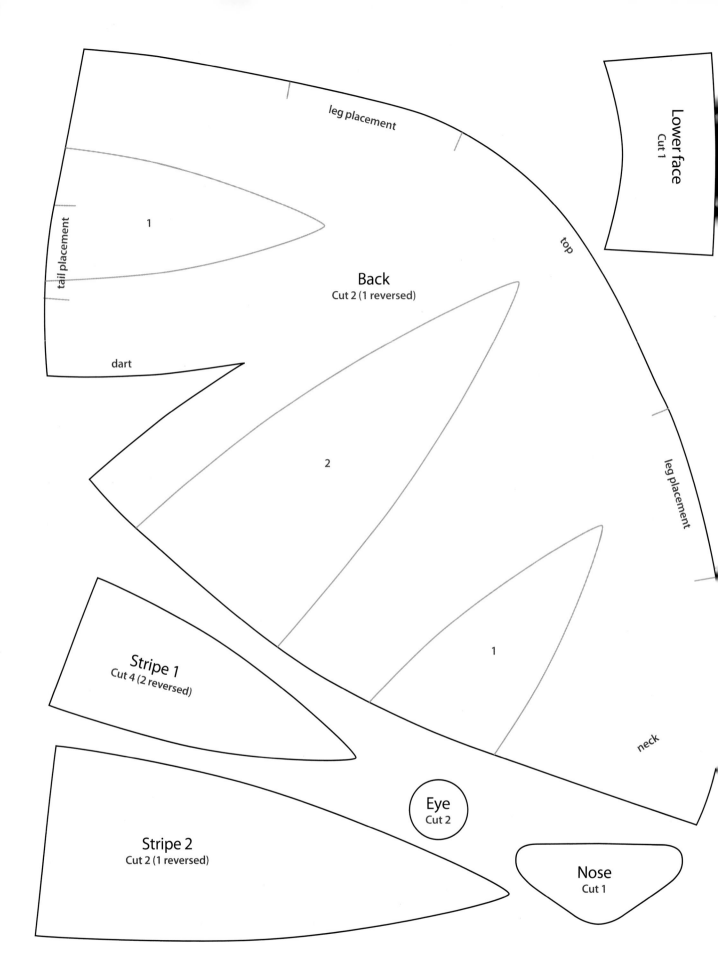

Lower face
Cut 1

leg placement

top

1

tail placement

Back
Cut 2 (1 reversed)

dart

2

leg placement

1

neck

Stripe 1
Cut 4 (2 reversed)

Eye
Cut 2

Stripe 2
Cut 2 (1 reversed)

Nose
Cut 1

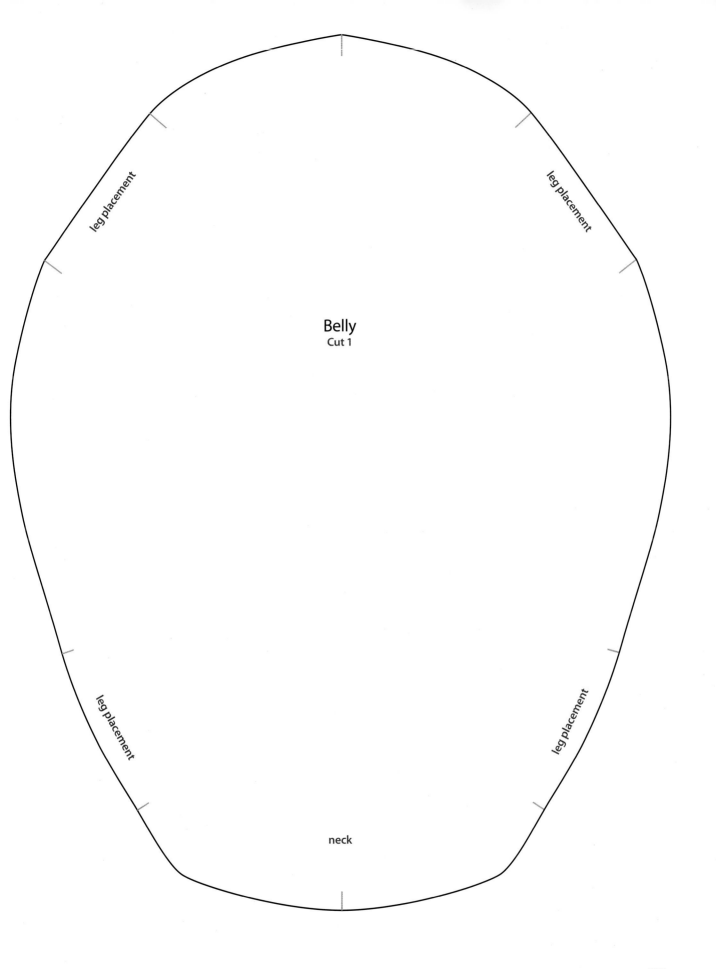

Belly
Cut 1

leg placement

leg placement

leg placement

leg placement

neck

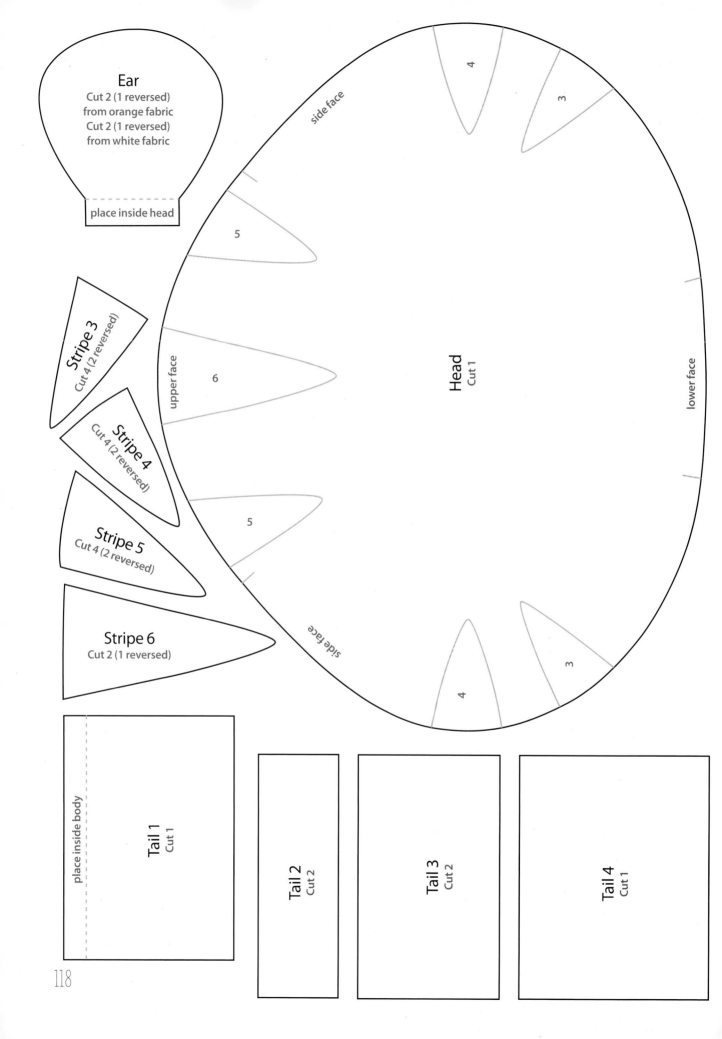

Ear
Cut 2 (1 reversed)
from orange fabric
Cut 2 (1 reversed)
from white fabric

place inside head

Head
Cut 1

side face

upper face

lower face

side face

4

3

5

6

5

4

3

Stripe 3
Cut 4 (2 reversed)

Stripe 4
Cut 4 (2 reversed)

Stripe 5
Cut 4 (2 reversed)

Stripe 6
Cut 2 (1 reversed)

place inside body

Tail 1
Cut 1

Tail 2
Cut 2

Tail 3
Cut 2

Tail 4
Cut 1

MARY THE HIPPO

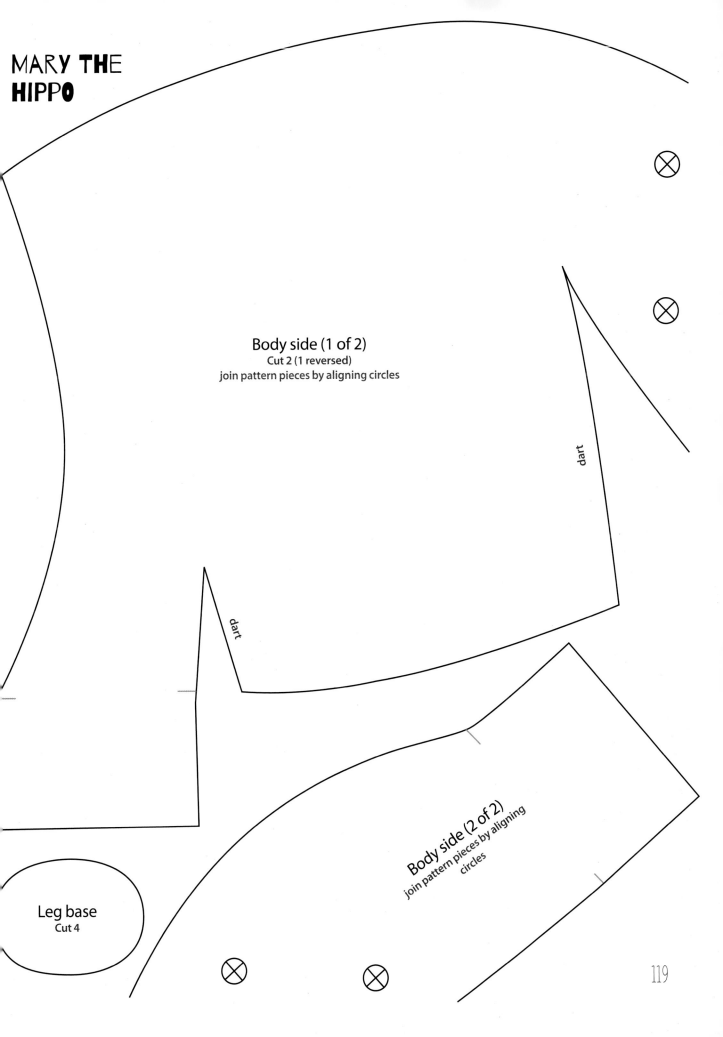

Body side (1 of 2)
Cut 2 (1 reversed)
join pattern pieces by aligning circles

dart

dart

Body side (2 of 2)
join pattern pieces by aligning circles

Leg base
Cut 4

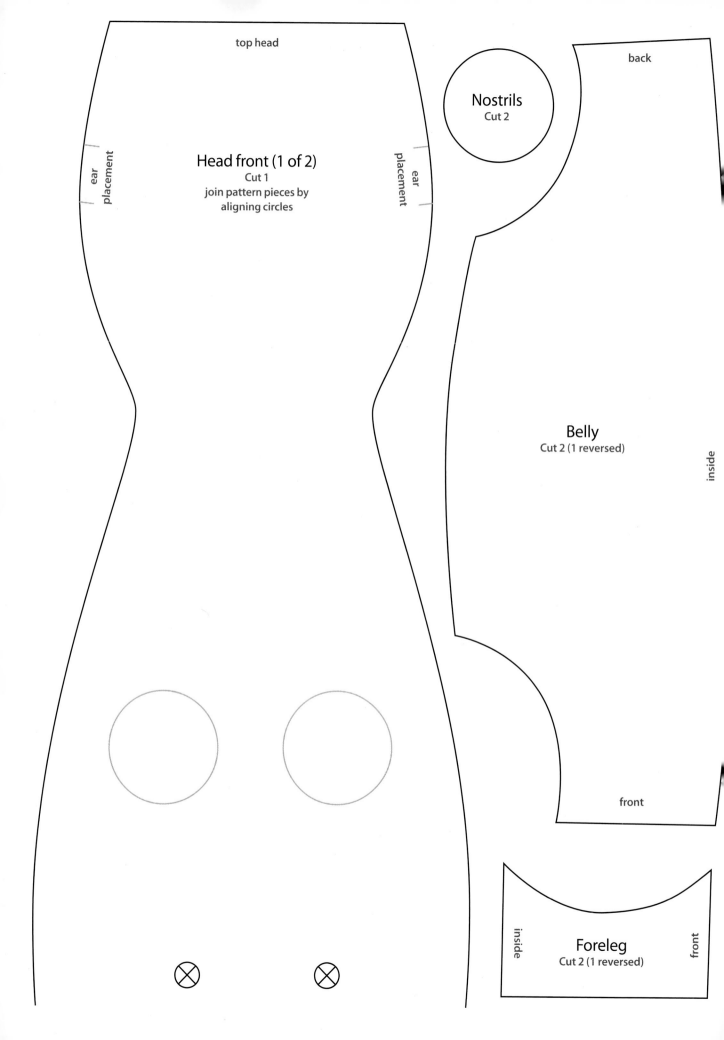

top head

Nostrils
Cut 2

back

ear placement

ear placement

Head front (1 of 2)
Cut 1
join pattern pieces by
aligning circles

Belly
Cut 2 (1 reversed)

inside

front

inside

Foreleg
Cut 2 (1 reversed)

front

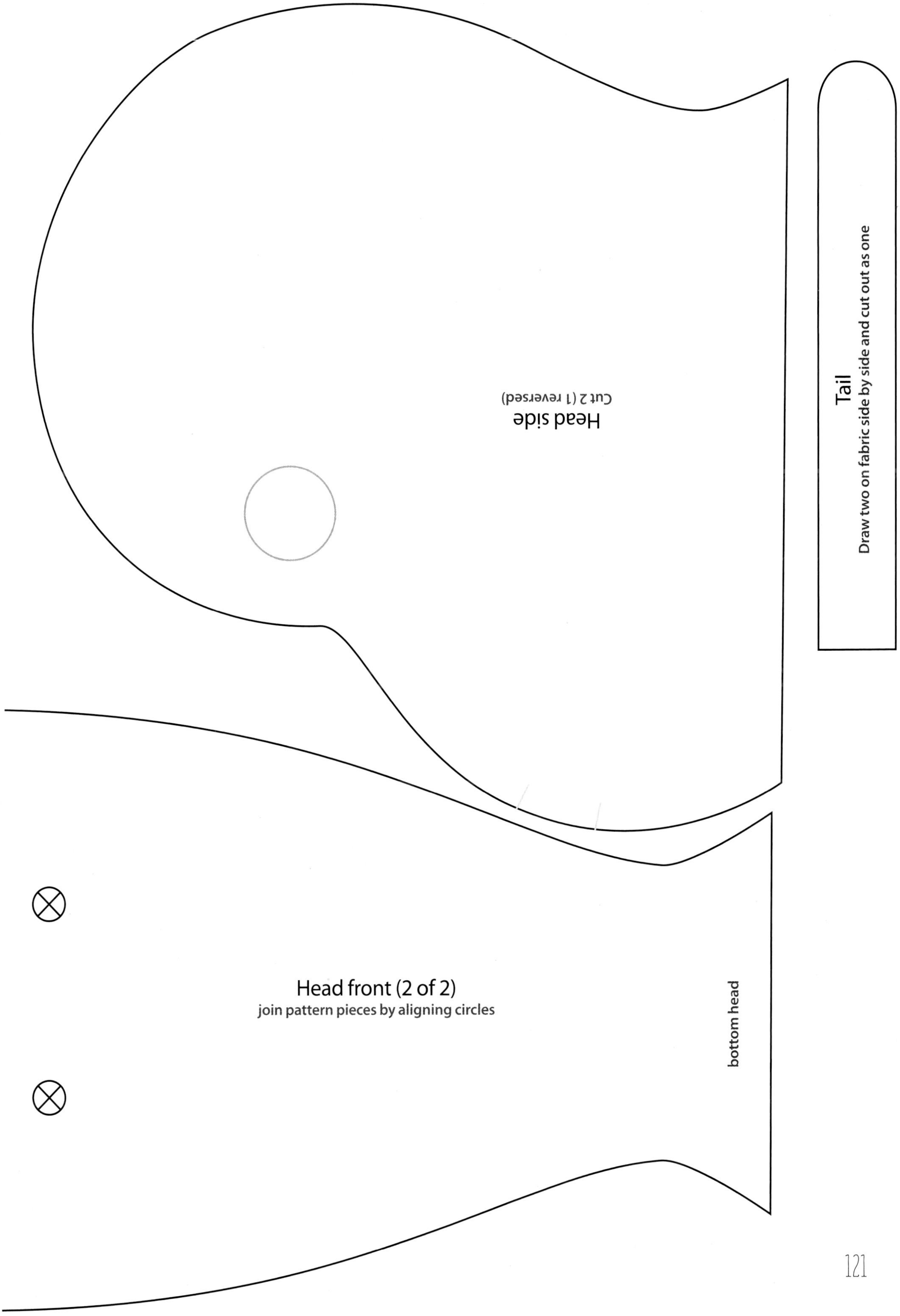

Head side
Cut 2 (1 reversed)

Tail
Draw two on fabric side by side and cut out as one

Head front (2 of 2)
join pattern pieces by aligning circles

bottom head

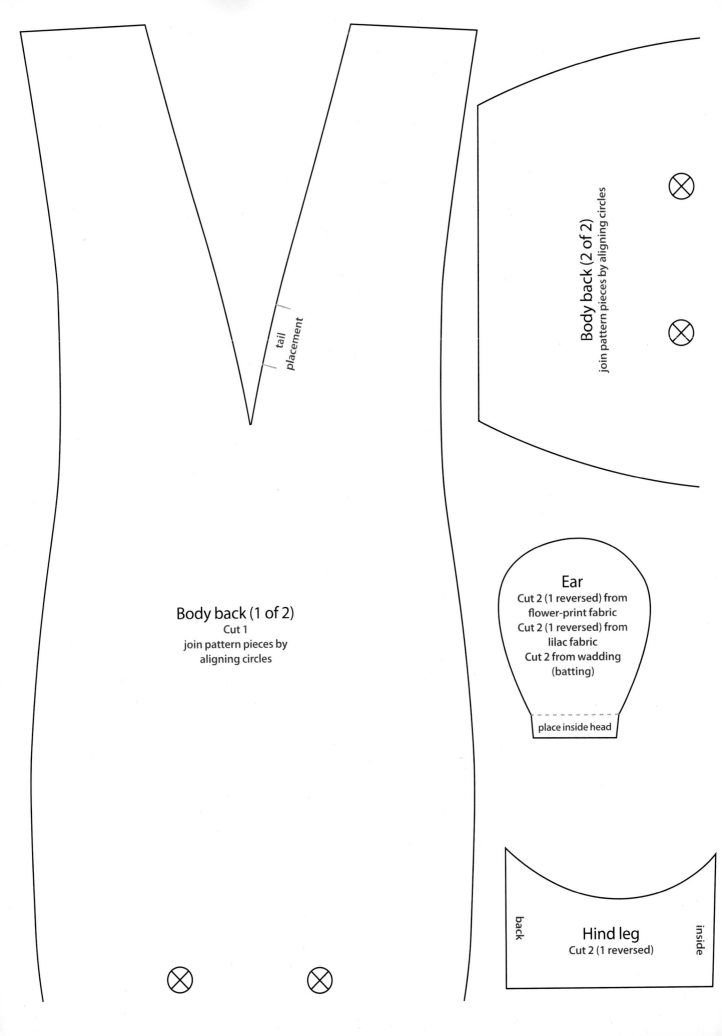

tail
placement

Body back (1 of 2)
Cut 1
join pattern pieces by
aligning circles

Body back (2 of 2)
join pattern pieces by aligning circles

Ear
Cut 2 (1 reversed) from
flower-print fabric
Cut 2 (1 reversed) from
lilac fabric
Cut 2 from wadding
(batting)

place inside head

back

inside

Hind leg
Cut 2 (1 reversed)

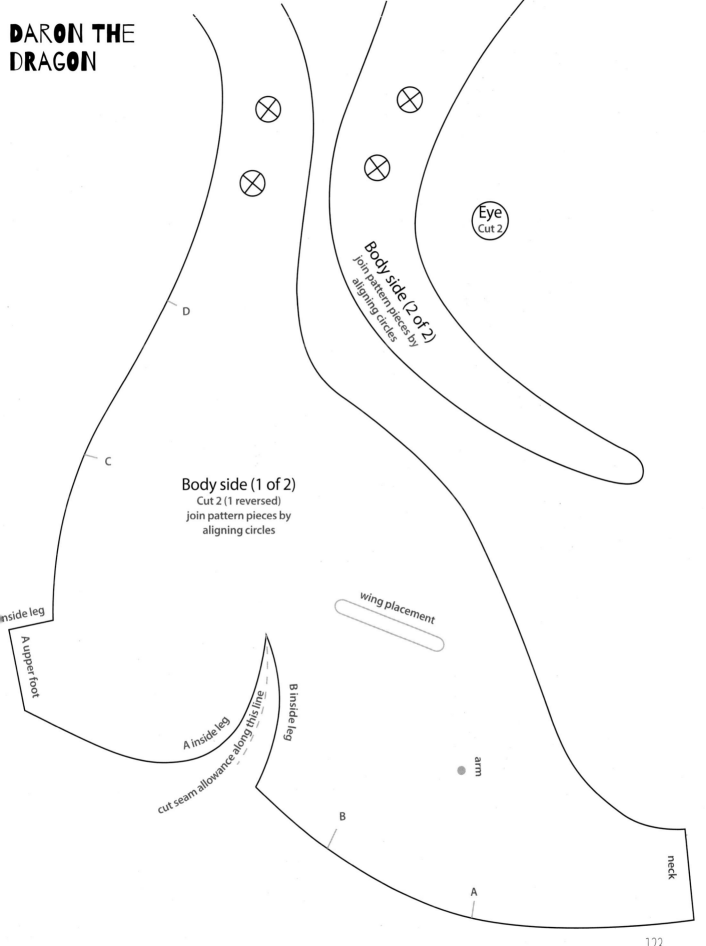

DARON THE DRAGON

Eye
Cut 2

Body side (2 of 2)
join pattern pieces by
aligning circles

D

C

Body side (1 of 2)
Cut 2 (1 reversed)
join pattern pieces by
aligning circles

inside leg

A upper foot

A inside leg

cut seam allowance along this line

B inside leg

wing placement

arm

B

neck

A

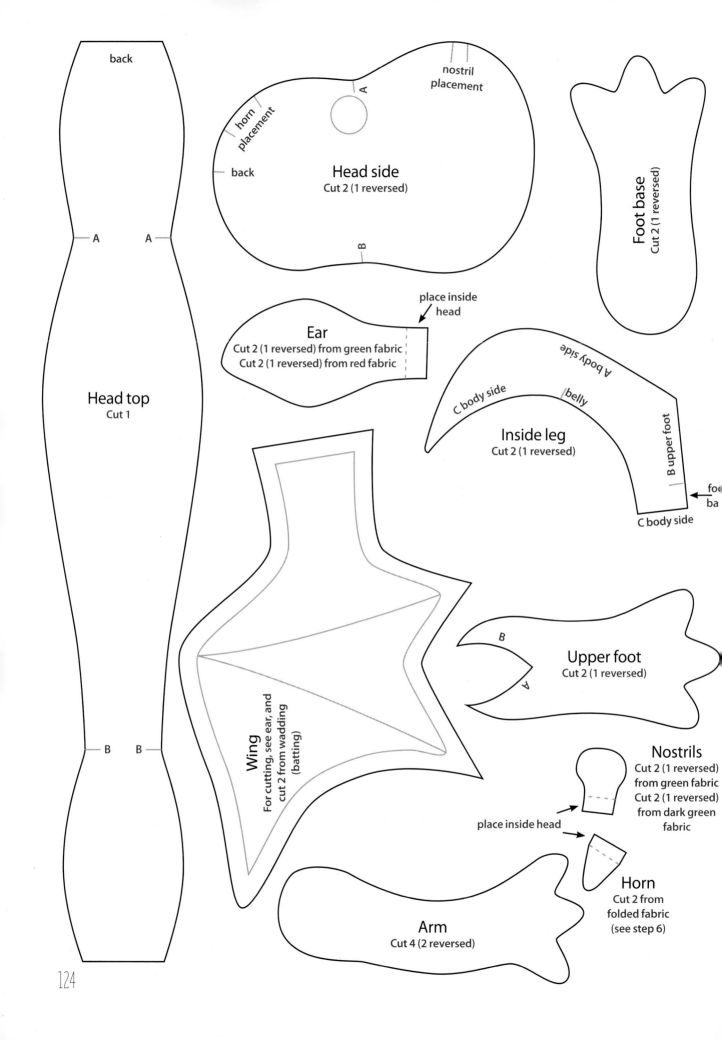

back

Head top
Cut 1

A   A

B   B

Head side
Cut 2 (1 reversed)

horn placement

back

nostril placement

A

B

Ear
Cut 2 (1 reversed) from green fabric
Cut 2 (1 reversed) from red fabric

place inside head

Wing
For cutting, see ear, and cut 2 from wadding (batting)

Foot base
Cut 2 (1 reversed)

Inside leg
Cut 2 (1 reversed)

A body side

C body side

belly

B upper foot

C body side

foot back

Upper foot
Cut 2 (1 reversed)

B

A

Nostrils
Cut 2 (1 reversed) from green fabric
Cut 2 (1 reversed) from dark green fabric

place inside head

Horn
Cut 2 from folded fabric (see step 6)

Arm
Cut 4 (2 reversed)

124

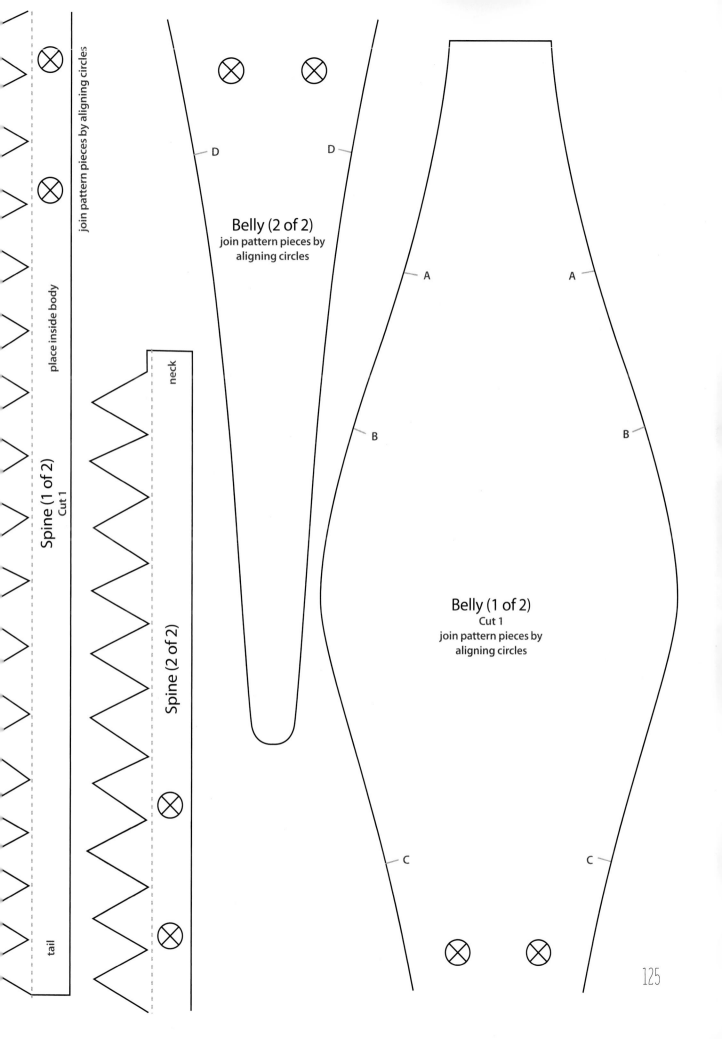

join pattern pieces by aligning circles

place inside body

Spine (1 of 2)
Cut 1

tail

neck

Spine (2 of 2)

Belly (2 of 2)
join pattern pieces by
aligning circles

D

D

A

A

B

B

Belly (1 of 2)
Cut 1
join pattern pieces by
aligning circles

C

C

ABOUT THE AUTHOR

Mariska Vos-Bolman is a graduate of the Utrecht School of Arts and she is the creator of the popular Fluffels and DIY Fluffies soft-toy brands, which are sold worldwide. She has been creative her whole life and bought her first sewing machine in 2006. Since then she has channelled most of her creativity into sewing plush toys. Her patterns are characterized by their cute and quirky style and their very detailed illustrated tutorials, which make them fun to create. Her work has been featured widely online, including high-profile blogs Craft Gossip and Handmadeology. She lives in Zaandam, The Netherlands.

www.mariskavos.nl

DIY Fluffies

ACKNOWLEDGMENTS

First of all I would like to thank my husband, Yannis, for supporting my dream and for his advice and help when creating my patterns. I would like to thank my mum, Tonnie, for helping me during the busy times — without her I wouldn't have had the time to make these patterns. I would also like to thank my publishers, David & Charles and F+W Media International team, for giving me the opportunity to make this book. Finally, a big thank you to all those people who have bought DIY Fluffies patterns and kits.

FABRIC SUPPLIERS

It is easy to source exciting fabrics online from all over the world at www.etsy.com or from www.dawanda.com (especially good for European fabric stores). Here are my own recommendations for sourcing colourful cotton fabrics online:

USA
Sew Fresh Fabrics
www.sewfreshfabrics.com
Pink Castle Fabrics
www.pinkcastlefabrics.com
Pink Chalk Fabrics
www.pinkchalkfabrics.com
The Fabric Fairy
www.thefabricfairy.com

NETHERLANDS
Online Stoffen
www.onlinestoffen.nl
(also good for fleece and felt)
Happy Stitches
www.happystitches.nl

UK
Sew and So
www.sewandso.co.uk
Swincraft2
www.stores.ebay.co.uk/Swincraft2
(particularly good for faux fur)
Fancy Moon
www.fancymoon.co.uk
My Fabric House
www.myfabrichouse.co.uk

AUSTRALIA
Earthgirl Fabrics
www.earthgirlfabrics.com.au

INDEX

A DAVID & CHARLES BOOK
© F&W Media International, Ltd 2014

David & Charles is an imprint of F&W Media International, Ltd
Pynes Hill Court, Pynes Hill, Exeter, EX2 5AZ, UK

F&W Media International, Ltd is a subsidiary of F+W Media, Inc
10151 Carver Road, Suite #200, Blue Ash, OH 45242, USA

Text and Designs © Mariska Vos-Bolman 2014
Layout and Photography © F&W Media International, Ltd 2014

First published in the UK and USA in 2014

A catalogue record for this book is available from the British Library.

ISBN-13: 978-1-4463-0486-0 paperback
ISBN-10: 1-4463-0486-8 paperback

Printed in China by RR Donnelley for:
F&W Media International, Ltd
Pynes Hill Court, Pynes Hill, Exeter, EX2 5AZ, UK

10 9 8 7 6 5 4 3

Acquisitions Editor: Ame Verso
Editor: Emma Gardner
Project Editor: Cheryl Brown
Designer: Jennifer Stanley
Photographers: Jack Kirby and Jack Gorman
Senior Production Controller: Kelly Smith

F+W Media publishes high quality books on a wide range of subjects. For more great book ideas visit:
www.sewandso.co.uk